God Hovered Over the Waters

God Hovered Over the Waters
The Emergence of the Protestant Reformation

William A. dePrater III

WIPF & STOCK · Eugene, Oregon

GOD HOVERED OVER THE WATERS
The Emergence of the Protestant Reformation

Copyright © 2015 William A. dePrater III. All rights reserved. Except for brief quotations in critical publications or reviews, no part of this book may be reproduced in any manner without prior written permission from the publisher. Write: Permissions. Wipf and Stock Publishers, 199 W. 8th Ave., Suite 3, Eugene, OR 97401.

Wipf and Stock
An Imprint of Wipf and Stock Publishers
199 W. 8th Ave., Suite 3
Eugene, OR 97401

www.wipfandstock.com

ISBN 13: 978-1-4982-0454-5

Manufactured in the U.S.A.   08/31/2016

To

Jacob Christopher
"Child of the Covenant"

Contents

Abbreviations | viii
Acknowledgments | ix

Introduction: Why Learn About the Reformation Era? | 1
1   Prelude to the Reformation | 5
2   Forerunners of the Protestant Reformation | 31
3   The Reformation in Germany | 45
4   The Reformation in Switzerland | 61

   Portraits of Reformers | 86

5   The Reformation in England, Scotland, Ireland, and Wales | 90
6   The Reformation in the Netherlands and France | 117
7   The Catholic Reformation | 126
8   The Legacy of the Protestant Reformation Today | 130

Appendix A: The Reformed Confessions | 143
Appendix B: Brief Timeline of Reformation Era Events | 146
Bibliography | 153
Index | 155

Abbreviations

CNS	Catholic News Service
CT	*Christianity Today*
CTQ	*Concordia Theological Quarterly*
LQ	*Lutheran Quarterly*
NIBC	New Interpreter's Bible Commentary
NIH	National Institute of Health
OJ	*Oxford Journal*
PC (USA)	Presbyterian Church (USA)
WTJ	*Westminster Theological Journal*

Acknowledgments

THE ORIGINS OF THIS book began almost forty-two years ago, when, as a newly ordained pastor, I began writing articles for church officer training. Since then, I have continued to convey to congregations our history as Presbyterians, and the substance of the doctrinal confessions to which we look for guidance. Since retirement in 2012, I have focused on the ministries of teaching and writing. Among those teaching opportunities, a series of classes that I conducted on the Protestant Reformation at the University Presbyterian Church in Chapel Hill, North Carolina, served as the initial inspiration for the writing of this book. In addition, a later teaching opportunity in the Duke University adult continuing education program helped in the shaping of the book's format. The creative point of interaction between the teaching and writing ministries hopefully will make the concepts expressed within this book more accessible to the reader.

I further wish to thank Wipf and Stock Publishers for their willingness to work alongside me in the publication of this book. Their interest in producing this book and their editorial guidance along the way were essential in its production.

Finally, I would like to thank my wife, Reverend Margaret Rogers dePrater, who tirelessly corrected my grammatical errors, and offered insightful editorial suggestions that greatly improved this book.

INTRODUCTION

Why Learn About the Reformation Era?

WHEN OUR YOUNGEST DAUGHTER gave birth to her first child and our first grandchild, my wife and I arrived at the hospital while she was in labor. Sitting anxiously in the hospital's maternity waiting room, we waited for news from the medical staff about our daughter and soon to be born grandchild. Finally, the news came! Our daughter was fine, and a new member of our family was born. His parents named him Jacob, one of the biblical patriarchs, and Christopher, which means "Christ-bearer." Further, being born on July 10, Jacob would share a birthday with John Calvin, the theological literary giant of the Reformation period. From the beginning of his life, his name and his birthday would remind him of the witness of those saints that have preceded him.

As soon as we first met Jacob, we began looking at his physical features—his long legs, his chubby cheeks, his sturdy frame, his almond-shaped eyes, and his hands and feet. We were excited when we recognized in him physical features similar to that of the members of his larger family. In so doing, we were bonding with him. We were claiming him as a family member. As he grows, he will continue to have characteristics that are similar to that of his parents, grandparents, aunts, and other family members, both the living and the dead. At the same time, he will be far different from anyone else that ever has lived. That is because Jacob is a unique person in his own right, with his own particular mixture of God-given gifts and graces that will enable him to live his life in faith. As he grows in wisdom and stature in facing the perils of childhood and the temptations of youth, he will become Jacob the man. He also will learn what it means to experience God's unbounded love in all of life's adventures.

In a similar manner, we have spiritual ancestors. Some of those spiritual ancestors we read about in the Scriptures: Abraham, Isaac, Jacob, Joshua, Joseph, the prophets, Paul of Tarsus, Timothy, Matthew, Mark, Luke, John, and of course Jesus. These stories tell us where we have come from as people of faith, how they faced their own life struggles, and how God established God's covenant with them and us.

We also have other spiritual ancestors whose names do not appear in the Scriptures. Their lives, likewise, have shaped us as Christians. These spiritual ancestors stepped out in faith, claimed God's vision for the future, and remained true to that vision against all opposition. I will share some of their stories in this book. Along with countless other unnamed women and men who faithfully served in congregations throughout the world, they are cheering us on in our Christian discipleship.

My hope for you as you read this book is fivefold: First, my hope is that I can kindle in you an appreciation of the struggles of these spiritual ancestors who have bequeathed to us the Reformed faith. Second, in such a short book, I certainly cannot pretend adequately to cover the lives of those who have gone before us. That is not been my intention. There are a number of scholarly books already on the market that have far more adequately achieved that task. My purpose therefore in writing this book is to introduce you to some of our ancestors in the faith, so that you might want to explore their lives further. Third, I have chosen to confine the time period to be covered in this book to that of the sixteenth and a portion of the seventeenth centuries. During the sixteenth century, the Reformers' faith was original, fresh, and groundbreaking. However, during the seventeenth century, Reformation leaders became more concerned with defending and codifying the Reformed doctrines and practices than with continuing the Reformed theological conversation. Orthodoxy became the standard of the faith, and the Reformed confessions increasingly became the means of gatekeeping within the community. Besides, with the writing of the Westminster Confession of Faith, the era of the great confessional documents passed into history. There are other fine confessional documents written in recent centuries, yet most of these confessional documents look back to the sixteenth and seventeenth century as the foundational confessional era.

Fourth, when I was a student in seminary in the early 1970s, there was great interest in the Consultation on Church Union (COCU), which was formed in 1962 under the leadership of Eugene Carson Blake, the stated clerk of the United Presbyterian Church USA, and Bishop James Pike of

Why Learn About the Reformation Era?

the Protestant Episcopal Church. With the overwhelming denominational rejection of the 1970 "Plan of Union," the Consultation on Church Union eventually dissolved. The organization named Churches Uniting in Christ (CUIC) succeeded it. Instead of COCU's original goal of organic union, CUIC advocated goals that are more modest. Since then, several ecumenical actions have taken place, including approval in the late 1970s of the CUIC's "Visible Marks of Churches Uniting in Christ," and the "Formula of Agreement between the Evangelical Lutheran Church in America, the Presbyterian Church (USA), the Reformed Church in America, and the United Church of Christ." Finally, in 2008 the General Assembly approved the "Covenant Relationship between the Korean Church in America and the PC (USA)." Other denominational traditions likewise have established similar relationships within their own communions. Yet, in the five hundred years since Martin Luther posted his "Ninety-Five Theses," the church continues to split asunder into ever-smaller denominations which are seeking unity through their uniformity of belief and practice. Martin Luther and the other Reformers never sought such divisions of Christ's Body, and they would be horrified at its extent today. Amidst that bitter period of religious estrangement, a Benedictine devotional writing, *Beneficio di Christo*, expressed the pain of such trauma:

> This may sound counted among the greatest evils with which this age is infected, that they which are called Christians are miserably divided about Christ; and yet in truth as the Apostle saith unto us, there is but one God, which is the Father, of whom are all things, and we in him, and our Lord Jesus Christ, by whom all things, and we by him. To discourse on this division, and to cause thereof would be to some pleasing; to some it would unpleasing. For what one truth can please minds so diversely divided? Would God it could please all to become one in that one Christ whose name we all do carry.[1]

At the same time, there are those churches who are seeking their unity not in polity and theology, but rather in the Christ and his calling to proclaim the gospel. These churches have been forming cooperative ecumenical relationships in communities large and small.

Fifth, in our celebration of our ecumenical relationships and common ministries, it is important that we have an understanding of the cultural, economic, ecclesiastical, and political circumstances that helped to usher

---

1. MacCulloch, *Reformation*, 707–8.

in the sixteenth-century Protestant Reformation. Only then can we affirm our own denominational traditions while following the Holy Spirit's lead in affirming: ". . . one Lord, one faith, one baptism, one God and Father of all, who is above all and through all and in all" (Eph 4:5). With the upcoming celebration of the five-hundredth anniversary of Martin Luther's posting of his "Ninety-Five Theses," my hope is that celebration will spur us onward in a continued dialogue of what it means for us to be the one Body of Christ.

1

Prelude to the Reformation

On March 11, 2011, from seventeen miles deep within the earth's crust, enormous forces drove convergent tectonic plates over another. In the collision, one plate riding over the other displaced massive amounts of water. The energy released in the collision of titans shook Japan with an 8.9-magnitude earthquake. Buildings shook in Japan, causing devastation. However, the worst was yet to come. The displaced water deep within the earth began racing toward the Japanese shoreline, each mile exponentially increasing in its fury. Racing ever faster, quickly it emerged from the deeper waters to the shallower Japanese continental shelf. Coming ashore in Japan as a thirty-foot-high wall of water, the tsunami swept aside everything in its path as if they were toys, thus destroying much of the nation's infrastructure, threatening the release of nuclear radiation throughout the world, and taking far too many lives. People felt aftershocks for days. In the year following, displaced relics of everyday Japanese life, once swept out to sea, and then pollution, crossed the Pacific Ocean and reached the western coast of the United States.

Similar to the 2011 tsunami, in sixteenth-century Europe there was a collision of changing forces: the political environment, the social unrest and the evolving socioeconomic social structures, the recovery from the effects of the bubonic plague, the development of an educated society, the invention of the printing press, the flowering of arts during the Renaissance, the differing interpretations of Scripture, and the spiritual yearning to know God. Like unto the energy created by colliding tectonic plates in 2011 that in a short time swept across major portions of Japan, the sixteenth-century collision of systemic forces enabled the Protestant Reformation to sweep across the face of Europe. From its meager beginnings with Wycliffe and

Huss, Luther's nailing of his "Ninety-Five Theses" to the church door at Wittenberg, the Protestant Reformation was swept up amidst the deep churning social and economic waters, finally emptying into theological lakes and streams across Europe. This theological tsunami changed the face of theology about the world. For us to understand the Protestant Reformation, we need to understand the dynamics within the Middle Ages in order to discover the systemic forces that were at play. All these factors helped lead to the emergence of the sixteenth-century Protestant Reformation. Let us therefore begin with the first tremors of the earthquake that was striking Europe.

Popular Unrest and Emerging Nationalism

The half-century encompassing 1450 to 1500 witnessed an era of unparalleled popular unrest and nationalism. Due to France's extended struggle with England (1339–1453), the power of the French nobility decreased and that of the French crown grew. Louis XI (1461–1483) broke the back of the feudal nobility and gave the crown unprecedented authority. His son, Charles VIII (1483–1498), led France in foreign conquests in Italy, and opened a new era in European international relationships, which determined the political background leading up to the Reformation era. Louis XII (1498–1515) and Francis I (1515–1547) extended these gains during their reigns, extending its control to the power of the church. By the dawn of the Protestant Reformation, the church in France was essentially a state-controlled church.

Spain, by the end of the fifteenth century, was unparalleled in the interwoven relationship of its national patriotism and Catholic orthodoxy. By the thirteenth century, the Moors were restricted to Granada, with four kingdoms created to provide order: Castile, Aragon, Portugal, and Navarre. Strong feudal nobility controlled each of these kingdoms, with limited national identity. The 1469 marriage of Ferdinand, the heir of Aragon, and Isabella, the heir of Castile, increased the power of the royal throne. Under their joint reign (1479–1504), royal authority was strengthened and the political aspirations of unruly feudal nobles were suppressed. The discovery of the New World by Columbus brought unimaginable wealth to the royal treasury. On Ferdinand's death in 1516, his grandson, the heir of Austria and the Netherlands, reigned as Charles V. Under Charles' leadership, Spain became a major world power.

Prelude to the Reformation

In England, the War of the Roses between the House of Lancaster and the House of York (1455–1485) claimed the power of the feudal nobility to the advantage of the royal crown and Parliament. Although Parliament retained certain legal responsibilities, Henry VII, the first king of the Tudor dynasty, assumed almost absolute power. By the close of the fifteenth century, the crown exerted considerable control over the English Catholic Church. The son of Henry VII, Henry VIII, in the sixteenth century, extended the power of the throne to provide state leadership of the church.

Lacking a real sense of unity, Germany was a very different political situation than which was found in the other leading European nations. From 1438-1740, the most powerful political force within Germany was the Austrian house of Habsburg. The reign of Frederick III (1440–1493), witnessed rivalry among the nobles and the cities, with the lower nobility keeping the land in disorder. Under the reign of Maximilian I (1493–1519), he unsuccessfully sought to increase royal power through the regional districts and the Reichstag. However, the imperial cities, accountable only to the emperor, and characterized by the self-seeking interests of their wealthy and industrious inhabitants, were an important political and economic ingredient in German life. Particularly in southwestern Germany, a constant state of popular unrest and rebellion existed. This unrest bubbled over with insurrections in 1476, 1492, 1512, and 1513. The establishment of Roman law, originally created to suppress the Roman slaves, exacerbated the political, economic, and social stress. In general, German national life was disorganized and dissatisfied, with dispersed power residing within the regional princes.

These princes in turn exerted considerable control over the church within their fiefdoms. A major transition occurred in the death of Charles the Bold. His daughter, Mary, inherited the Burgundian territories and the Netherlands. Following her marriage, in the following year, to Maximilian I of Germany, Louis XI of France, in showing his dissatisfaction over the marriage, seized upper Burgundy. Until 1756, his actions forthwith would be the backdrop for the constant quarrels between the House of Habsburg and the French kings. However, in seeking reconciliation, Maximilian and Mary's son Philip married Juana, the daughter of Ferdinand and Isabella. Philip and Juana's son, Charles V of Spain, possessed Austria, the Netherlands, and the Spanish territories in Europe and the New World. In 1519, he would assume the title of Holy Roman Emperor.

The Disorienting and Transforming Effects of Disease

The Black Death

During the Middle Ages and Early Modern Europe, death was always the unacknowledged elephant in the room. The bubonic plague was the major cause of death, which people also called "the Black Death." The disease first manifested itself with tumors in the lymph glands of the groin or armpits. Some of these tumors grew as large as an apple or egg. Soon the disease began to spread throughout the body, producing black spots on the arms, thighs, or elsewhere. The skin and flesh soon would turn black and then die. Its victims died a frustrating and painful death within one to three days. There also was another form of the plague, which affected the lungs and eventually choked its victims to death. People therefore referred to it as the "pneumonic plague." The Black Death first appeared in 1347 at the trading city of Caffa in the Crimea. The bubonic plague last struck in a substantial form in 1721 at the Mediterranean port of Marseille, France. It began its deadly travels near China and journeyed along the Silk Road, carried by Mongol armies, traders, or ships. Its effects were devastating to those it touched. People died by the hundreds. Day and night, workers threw corpses into newly dug trenches and covered them with earth. One at that time woman wrote that she buried her five children with her own hands. Many thought that these deaths were signaling the end of the world. In fact, during its protracted siege of Caffa, the Mongol army suffered greatly from the plague. To weaken the resolve of the defenders of Caffa, the Mongol army catapulted their infected dead over the city walls. Terror quickly seized the defenders. The traders soon fled the city, taking with them the disease by ship into Sicily and south of Europe. From there, the plague spread north into Europe.

The plague did not claim its victims in any uniform manner throughout Europe. Rather, geography influenced the extent of the plague. In 1466, as many as 400,000 people died of the plague in Paris. In the Mediterranean region, particularly in Italy, the south of France, and in Spain, the plague ran rampant for four consecutive years. During that time, it killed close to 75 percent of the population. In Germany and England, it probably killed about 20 percent. During the sixteenth and seventeenth centuries, the plague visited its terror upon Paris three times. It ravaged London six times between 1563 and 1665, reducing the population by up to 30 percent. In all, the plague likely killed about one third of the European population.

Many people blamed the foreigners and Jews for the plague, and in their bias they burned alive these innocents. In August 1349, the people exterminated the Jewish communities in Mainz and Cologne. That same year, the citizens of Strasbourg murdered 2,000 Jews. The reason that many people blamed the Jews for the bubonic plague was that the Jewish communities experienced a lower manifestation of the plague than among the Christian communities. Perhaps one explanation of the different degrees of plague manifestation was that the Jews kept more cats around their houses than did Christians. Christians had not kept the protective cats, as they associated cats with witchcraft. This is one more case where ignorance and superstition aggravated great suffering and was the seedbed of great injustices in our history. In addition to the plague, diseases such as syphilis, smallpox, typhus, and influenza were widely feared. However, the plague struck terror into every heart.

There were systemic social and economic forces that enabled the plague to spread throughout the populace:

- People did not recognize the importance of hygiene until the nineteenth century. As a result, city streets were filthy, with farm animals being unrestrained and human parasites running rampant. The rat flea that carried the bubonic plague found a host in the rats, which lived amidst this filth. The rat fleabite rapidly spread the disease from infected rats to humans.

- Another factor that contributed to the outbreak of the plague was the significant climate change that was taking place. The warmer climate that had existed during the medieval period suddenly changed toward the end of the thirteenth century, with much colder years. The harsher climate thereupon reduced food harvests. The resulting food shortages brought about inflated prices, especially with oats and hay. The inflated prices of feed in turn reduced the supply of livestock that one could raise. In turn, the food shortage increased human malnutrition, with the resulting increased infection rates due to weakened immune systems.

- Family planning was non-existent. Women gave birth to five or more children during their lifetime, causing an increasing strain on the food supply.

- In addition, people were poor stewards of the land, cutting the forests, draining the swamps, and indiscriminately plowing the fields. This poor care of the environment reduced land for the grazing of farm animals. With the uncontrolled cutting of the forests, there was a reduced renewable source of firewood. With the reduction in livestock, their manure, which farmers used for fertilizer, also became scarce. It was a vicious cycle. The poor use of environmental resources caused unexpected consequences resulting in the outbreak of the plague and its horrors. Nevertheless, over time the environment and its inhabitants began to regain an environmental balance. Following the initial outbreaks of the Black Death and the resulting famines, people began to assert family planning and economic reforms. They developed trade routes so that they would be able to import grain from the thinly populated regions of eastern Europe. Further, the population began to live within their means. As a result, land became more plentiful. Forests began to grow back. This rebalancing of the environment did not happen overnight. It would take several generations before nature could repair the damages that humanity had inflicted upon the environment.

Syphilis and Influenza

Around the year 1510, the changing face of Europe began to coalesce. That year saw the first slave revolt on Hispaniola, the first description of a Christmas tree, the first pocket watches, as well as pretzel bows and Benedictine liquor. Protestants likewise would remember 1510 as the year when John Calvin was born. Only eighteen years before his birth, Columbus had discovered the "New World" and brought back tales of new peoples and strange foods and animals. The sailors also brought back new and terrible diseases such as syphilis. However, by 1510 Europe was beginning to recover slowly from the Black Death and the effects of syphilis.

Then another disease struck Europe in July and August of that same year. A new and even more sinister disease, known as influenza, struck with a fury. It had been around various regions for about 650 years, with strains perhaps having existed as far back as the ninth century. Its effects were coughing, high fever, and a tendency to develop deadly pneumonia. In September of 1510, King Louis XII convened a meeting of bishops, prelates, and university professors, yet they had to adjourn the meeting when the disease without warning struck its participants. Fortunately, the influenza burned itself out as quickly as it had struck, with deaths mostly occurring in children, the elderly, pregnant women, those with weakened immune systems, as well as those patients who had been bled excessively by their physicians.

The attacks of influenza in 1510 and later in 1557 and 1580 were the first recorded pandemics. Physicians at the time generally had no understanding of the concept of infection, instead thinking that they had to remove the "ill humors" in the blood through bleeding their patients. In addition, they sought to heal their patients through inducing vomiting and diarrhea, and blistering the skin. Such well-meaning practices only served to weaken further their ill patients. Girolamo Fracastoro in 1546 suggested that ill patients might be transmitting the disease to new victims. However, he failed to grasp that the medical world was fighting a disease that kept recurring in various strains. People referred to influenza by different names, including "catarrhal headaches," "poppy" due to the opiates used to treat it, "fifth cough," and "hoods," probably due to patients wearing hoods over their heads. While physicians struggled to identify the disease and treat their patients, Pope Julius II (1443–1513) could only suggest that the illness was due to human sins. Influenza was responsible for the loss of about 1 percent of the population, the same as for the later "Spanish Flu," which struck in 1918. The invention of the printing press and moveable type led to the sharing of information among physicians and as a result slowly advanced medical knowledge about treating influenza and other diseases.

England: A Template for Medieval Medical Care

In England, medical care had two benchmarks, the years of 1348 and 1518. The first date was the onset of the second pandemic of the bubonic plague. The plague struck not only patients, but likewise physicians, medical teachers, and medical authors, inflicting blows from which the medical community never recovered. Physicians felt helpless in the face of the overwhelming pandemic, relying on medical knowledge gained from the writings of Greek and Arabic physicians dating from five hundred to a thousand years prior to the fourteenth century. Due to the limited success of general practice physicians in providing cures to the bubonic plague, the public turned to surgeons and barber-surgeons for their medical care. Likewise, injuries incurred during the wars from 1346 to 1514 provided battlefield surgeons with opportunities to try new surgical techniques without interference from the church or civil authorities. Following the war, the royal courts employed the more successful surgeons as personal physicians.

Henry V, an admirer of surgeons' skills, in 1423 approved the founding of the College of Medicine and the later London-based Fellowship of Surgeons. However, the opportunities for surgical clinical practice began to diminish after 1450 due to a reduction in military campaigns as well as the development of new surgical techniques.

In 1518, the second of the medieval medical benchmarks, Henry VIII, desiring to improve medical care, established the Royal College of Physicians. Having little confidence in surgeons, he excluded them from the new organization. By 1530, the English medical establishment was in a condition of inertia. Few physicians learned their craft through clinical practice, and, with the Black Death no longer a pandemic, they developed a sense of complacency. Although some argue that the establishment of the Royal College of Physicians was an important benchmark in the evolution of modern medicine, physicians such as Robert Gottfried argue that the establishment of the College marked the end of innovation and discouraged clinical practice as a means of gaining medical knowledge. At the same time, the 170 years between the two benchmarks in medieval medical care—the devastation of the Black Death and the establishment of the Royal College of Physicians—were some of the most innovative years in medical advancement. Italian physicians, as well as innovative new techniques by battlefield surgeons, became the inspiration for the seventeenth-century physician William Harvey's groundbreaking work on the circulatory system.

Throughout these years, medieval doctors inherited two distinct traditions in their theory and practice. One tradition they inherited was from the Greeks, particularly the works of Hippocrates and Galen. Due to the church's influence, many of these writings disappeared from the public realm in the early Middle Ages; however, they were welcomed in the Islamic world. With the coming of the twelfth century, the return of these historic documents included additional commentaries by skilled Islamic physicians. The theoretic basis of Greek-Arabic medical knowledge was the concept of logic, rather than that of clinical practice. Physicians using the Greek theory of body humors treated their patients with changes in diet, bleeding their patients to remove the ill humors, and primitive medications. The second medical tradition was more pragmatic—that of folk medicine. Throughout northern Europe, these practitioners used herbs and performed some surgeries. Their emphasis on learning from clinical practice contrasted with that of the theoretical basis gained from the Greeks. In time, with the Norman invasion and the establishment of universities, which adopted the Greek model, the influence of folk medicine began to wane. Nevertheless, knowledge gained through folk medicine was included in the practice of some surgeons, barber-surgeons, and within the Benedictine monastic communities.

The Evolving Socioeconomic Structures

The Privileged Social Classes and Tax Exemption

In most of Europe, tax exemption was granted to two privileged classes—the nobility and the clergy. They justified their exemption due to the two prevalent concepts of labor. That is, the noblemen fought the wars at great personal expense, and at times gave their lives for the security of the people. In turn, the priests prayed and gave up worldly pleasures for the salvation of the people. Therefore, it was felt that the state should reward financially those persons serving in these professions. Peasants, merchants, and artisans, moreover, had the duty to provide for their financial support through taxation.

Despite their attempts to justify why they should not pay taxes, there was considerable objection to paying the required tithe to the bishop. The following conversation perhaps took place in 1320 regarding the payment of such a tithe. Five peasants were sitting under an elm tree in the village square. One remarked, "We're going to have to pay the bishop's tax on the new born lambs." "Don't let us pay anything," answered one of the others. "Let us rather find one hundred livres to pay two men to kill the bishop." "I'll willingly pay my share," replied the third man. "Money could not be better spent."[1]

Occasionally, armed rebellions took place against the privileged nobility. The nobles' response to such rebellions was to use violence to shatter resistance. Only the nobility also knew how to use the sword and pistol, and they freely used them whenever they felt threatened. Even when the nobility were in the wrong, the courts refused to punish them. The nobility rarely accounted for more than 2 percent of the population, and yet they possessed nearly 50 percent of the land in some regions, with all the wealth and power that it brought.

By the seventeenth century, newcomers to the nobility class had emerged. They desired to possess the privileges and recognition that the nobility had received. They literally came to blows over which one of them

---

1. Huppert, *After the Black Death*, 56–57.

would be entitled to sit in the front seats of the church. A country priest once wrote, "They are like pigs, they tear each other up. They have nothing but contempt for each other; they think that they can add weight to their own reputation by accusing others of being more recent nobility."[2] Such privilege required the possession of great wealth and the appearance of being noble. In order to maintain their appearance of being in the nobility, the new social class strictly observed social etiquette, including the social privilege of wearing of silk hose and carrying firearms.

The Difficulties of Life within the Peasant Villages

About 80 percent of the population lived in peasant villages, with generally about five hundred to seven hundred people comprising the average village. Bread was the staple diet, along with the raising of cattle and pigs for meat and tending fruit orchards, which supplied apples, pears, plums, and chestnuts. Further, there were garden vegetables, fish in ponds, and bees for honey and wax. Homes were thatch-roofed with two rooms, an attic, a barn, and a cowshed. The village was a very self-sufficient unit.

The residents of these villages had the distinctive physical characteristics of stunted growth and a yellowish complexion. By the time children were ten to twelve years old, they had assumed the physical characteristics of their elders. With distended bellies, they moved slowly, and all had poor oral hygiene. Women did not have menstruation until eighteen years of age. All of these characteristics were the result of poor nutrition.

One third of the infants died in their first year, and only one third of children reached adulthood. Most couples had only one or two children before one of the partners died. Women married at about twenty-three years of age, with the death of their partner occurring within ten years. When a spouse died, due to economic circumstances, widows and widowers remarried very soon. As their resources could not support more than two generations at a time, most people did not marry until after the last of their parents had died. Pragmatically, marriage was an economic decision, not a romantic decision. Often, the number of sheep a bride could bring as a dowry into a marriage was the key factor in such decisions. In addition, the community cared for orphans, as they were a source of financial capital and could be an important part of the labor force.

2. Ibid., 63.

Prelude to the Reformation

The Inequalities of Village Society

Life was very difficult within the peasant villages. The more financially secure farmers owned a team of horses and a plow. They leased their farms from absentee property owners. In France, people referred to this social class as *laboureurs* and in England as "yeomen." Even though they lived just this side of poverty, their lives appeared wealthy to the lower social classes. The "renters" (*laccataires*) did not own horses or plows—these tenant farmers were in constant danger of losing the land they rented. The "artisans" lived in the village center, often above their shops. They consisted of the smiths, miller, and innkeeper. They held influence in the village due to their dealing with goods and money. The "hired hands" (*journaliers*) owned nothing except their home, and a pig.

The "outsiders" lived on the fringes of society, and yet by owning property they constituted the local elite. This included the priest, notary, business agent, estate manager, and wealthy gentlemen.

The house of the priest was the most imposing in the village and included a chapel. The priests lived comfortably on rents and tithes assigned to the church. Many priests were not educated, so they did not understand Latin, and thus simply committed the Mass to memory. The church leadership was not troubled over their lack of understanding, as they felt that one did not need to understand Latin, as long as the priest said the words correctly. In turn, the people did not know Latin, and therefore could not understand the phrases that their priest was saying in his consecrating the elements. As a result, superstition arose. For example, the phrase "Hocus Pocus" is a corruption of the phrase "This is my body" in Latin, "*Hoc est corpus meum.*" Frequently, as priests were poorly educated, they left preaching to specialists such as the Dominicans, who were traveling monks. At the best, a priest visited the families in his parish every three years. Priests assigned to urban congregations frequently were more educated than those whom the bishop assigned to rural congregations. Yet bishops were not much better in their theological knowledge and professional conduct. The popes had appointed them from affluent families, and many had not received a theological education prior to their assuming office. Frequently, the popes increased their income through the buying and selling of such church offices, allowing several people to hold multiple church offices at the same time. Likewise, some bishops lived outside of their diocese, simply collecting their salaries without providing any ecclesiastical services. As corruption at times even extended to the pope, therefore there was not any means to make significant reformation within the system. It would take a grassroots effort to bring about change. By the 1400s, such a movement had begun to arise from some of the monastic orders.

The "notary" was essential in a society in a time in which illiteracy was widespread. Along with the business agent and the estate manager, they represented the absentee landowners. Yet they also owned property. The wealthy "gentlemen" visited the villages occasionally in the summer or during hunting season. Each of them owned several farms, which they leased out to the villagers.[3]

There were great extremes of wealth and poverty in the villages. The more prosperous farmers might have some reserves of bacon and cheese, a wardrobe full of clothes, and bedding to keep them warm on cold nights. In contrast, the landless peasants and the artisans were living in severe poverty, in cold, dark cottages with only the clothes on their backs, and frequently knowing hunger. Yet, there was no strife within the village against the social structures—all because there was no one in the villages to provide leadership. Each family was on its own for survival. "These seventeenth-century peasant families are as isolated and as unstable as are modern families of wage earners living in impersonal housing projects on the periphery of industrial cities." [4]

Agriculture, Acts of God, and the Church

As agriculture was the primary means of producing income, it had to be a collective enterprise. Therefore, the crops were planted and gathered according to an agreed upon schedule, with neighbors helping neighbors in the process. Likewise, the entire community suffered when there was a crop failure, due to warring armies, too much rain, too little rain, or other weather-related causes. These so-called "acts of God" people understood as God's punishment for a family's sin. Excommunication frequently was the church's response for such sin. Only as one can gain an appreciation of the communal nature of medieval society can one begin to understand the social impact of the church's act of excommunication. Excommunication was not only a matter of social disgrace, but also an act that prevented one from participating in community life. For example, one who was

---

3. Ibid., 3–5.
4. Ibid., 5.

excommunicated could not receive the Eucharist, act as a godparent, or be buried in a consecrated cemetery.

Although many people resented their priest's failure to provide their pastoral responsibilities, people loved their particular congregation and its sanctuary. They diligently maintained the buildings that their ancestors had built. Yearly religious-social ceremonies would bring out the entire village, with Masses being more of a social occasion than a religious one. There also were male social clubs in the villages that provided solidarity beyond the family. These social clubs supported festivals in conjunction with the church ceremonies.

The Privileges of Life within the Urban City

Those cities with populations of 10,000 to 30,000 inhabitants were surrounded with massive stone walls to keep out outsiders. As they lived off the goods produced in the rural areas, these urban dwellers ate well and dressed well without the need for plowing or herding. Supplies of grain, wine, oil, and salted pork were plentiful. The urban city was a privileged closed society, with a curfew at which time they drove vagrants outside the city walls. Over the city gates, they hung on iron stakes the severed heads of executed criminals. The city dwellers closely guarded their wealth. Cities with populations of 100,000 or more persons frequently imported provisions from throughout the world. The easy portability of money for financial transactions enabled buying and selling of goods from far away.

By the sixteenth century, European cities had recovered from the Black Death, and their structures extended beyond the city walls. The cities of Naples and Paris each reached a population of 200,000. Venice, Milan, Genoa, Florence, Lisbon, Rome, Palermo, Seville, Madrid, London, Antwerp, and Amsterdam all reached 100,000.

The citizens excluded the poor and the foreigner from the city. The poor could not pay taxes and did not have regular employment. The poor composed about 10 percent of the population, with servants making up to 20 percent of the population. The foreigner might include those persons who lived no more than an hour's walk from the city. Residents might become citizens if they met certain requirements, including a residency of one to ten years, a one-time residency initiation fee, and ownership of a house or payment of a certain amount of rent. In order to become a citizen, the law required one to unite with a local congregation. In this way, Catholics excluded Protestants in Catholic cities, and Protestants excluded Catholics in Protestant cities.

Persecution of the Jews

Augustine of Hippo in his writings had struggled with how Christians should relate to Jews within the cities. Against Christian extremists that rejected the Hebrew Scriptures, Augustine taught that God had chosen the Jews as a warning against such Christians. In God's plan, he felt, at Christ's second coming the Jews would convert to Christianity en mass. He taught that people, in the meanwhile, should not persecute the Jews in their communities. Citizens should allow them to live peacefully within their own communities, even though the authorities should not allow them the privilege of full citizenship.

Officially, rulers generally followed Augustine's guidance in protecting Jewish communities. An exception was Edward I of England, who in 1290 expelled all Jews from England. From that point onward, the only Jews that the English people could envision were theatrical actors portraying Jews as villains and Christ-haters and crucifers. Given the propaganda promoted by the social media, few persons could even have comprehended that Jesus had lived his life as a faithful Jew. Facing persecution throughout Europe, Jews sought to blend into the native cultures. They spoke the language of their neighbors and sought not to stand out in public. Italian rulers encouraged Jewish residents to live in certain areas of cities for their own safety. The word "ghetto," in fact, comes from an Italian word descriptive of such Jewish communities. All the while, Jews worshipped in their synagogues and used the ancient Hebrew language in worship and in the reading of the Scriptures. Tragically, in some places, church authorities continued to encourage anti-Semitic violence. Among the religious orders, the Franciscans and their rivals the Dominicans particularly promoted violence against Jewish communities.

Symptoms of Social Unrest

Prior to getting married, people were dependent on their parents. Ordinances forbade women who were under fifty years old from establishing their own household. Instead, they required them to share a home with an older single woman. The craft guild frequently arranged marriages for such single women. Further, there was a pecking order among the various craft guilds. Even so, there was a large number of unmarried women within the cities.

Social unrest was evident in the sexual tension between the older men with mistresses and the younger men who lived at home and were dependent on their parents. Groups of these young men, between the ages of eighteen and twenty-four, who were the sons of journeymen and servants frequently raped young women. Usually the victim was a servant girl that had slept with her master, a priest's lover, a young widow, or a wife whose husband was away on business or a military campaign. Such gangs were abrasive, frequently breaking down doors of homes and raping the women inside. The city leaders responded to the frequency of rapes by opening certified houses of prostitution. Some bishops encouraged young priests either to have lovers or to visit these brothels. Of course, since it was illegal under church law for them to engage in such sexual activity, they had to pay a fine each year to the bishop. There further were convents in Rome that served as brothels for priests to visit. Bishops were not much better in their conduct. Once Luther referred to some church cardinals as "saints" since they went after adult women and not children. Certified prostitutes were required to pay a fee and secure a license. They were permitted to wear a badge signifying that they were licensed prostitutes and therefore under the protection of the law. When they reached the age of twenty, certified prostitutes would begin working in bathhouses, in which there was more sexual activity than bathing. Still later, they would work in brothels. When prostitutes retired at thirty years of age, city leaders would find them husbands and grant them a dowry.

The Evolution of the Rentiers Social Class

Slowly, significant changes began coming to the urban city. A new, highly educated social class composed of law school–educated civil servants, called "rentiers," began to emerge. The term "rentiers" came from the loans ("rentes") they issued, at 10 percent interest, to starving peasants or unfortunate men needing quick cash. In time, through these "rentes" they accumulated substantial financial wealth. They even loaned money to the government at 8.3 percent annually. These rentiers had realized that education was the means for upward mobility within the city social and economic structure. Accumulating financial power, they seized control of city government and saw to it that the government granted them exemption from taxation. In turn, they acquired public office and became bishops, abbots, and ministers of state.

The Role of Faith in Medieval Society

The Monastic Movement, the Papacy, and Church Architecture

The Monastic Movement

Despite the criticism that they received, the monasteries and the papacy were the two institutions that provided for social and economic order during the Middle Ages. The monastic orders, founded by the Eastern church, based in Constantinople, focused primarily on the contemplative renunciation of sins and the life of prayer. In contrast, the monastic orders founded in the Western church, based in Rome, focused primarily on serving the larger community. One such means of community service was the copying and preserving of manuscripts for later generations. Further, the land owned by the monasteries in time began to have an economic stimulus within the economy due to the diligent labor of the monks. Later during the thirteenth century, orders such as the Franciscans and Dominicans embraced poverty as a saintly lifestyle. Like the Benedictine order, the Franciscans and Dominicans also embraced scholarship, recruiting many of their members from persons with academic training, and they became prominent in founding universities and holding professorships. It was from these newer monastic orders that both the proponents and opponents of the Protestant Reformation movement developed. The traveling friars had closer contact with the needs of the people due to their dependence on their financial support, with preaching and hearing of confessions as their primary activities. In time, there began to be competition between the parishes and the monastic orders over the offering given by the people. As a result, there were occasions when ecclesiastical conflict flared up. Traveling friars referred to parish priests as lazy and ignorant, while parish priests referred to friars as showmen trying to entice attractive women into their confessionals. Friars likewise sneered at monks as being useless consumers of the offerings of the wealthy landed class.

Prelude to the Reformation

The Papacy

The second institution that gave order during the Middle Ages was the papacy. Although there are various lists of bishops of Rome dating from the late second century, these lists do not agree. Some scholars have suggested that there may have been for some time a "collegial episcopacy." Over time, the bishop of Rome assumed a primary role in the church. Some have suggested that the impetus may have occurred during the mid-fifth century due to the barbarian invasions. From that time forward, it became the guardian of the values of Western civilization. Perhaps the most capable of the early bishops of Rome was Gregory "the Great." Born in Rome in about 540, he learned as a Roman public official effectively how to constructively use power. Upon his being elected as bishop of Rome (590–604), he immediately set himself to the task of facing the challenges posed by the Black Death: distributing food to the hungry, guaranteeing regular shipments of wheat from Sicily, seeing that drinkable water was brought to Rome through the rebuilding of the aqueduct systems, and the strengthening of the military defenses. A prolific writer, he credited Augustine, bishop of Hippo, as shaping his theological thinking. Yet he went far beyond Augustine's assertions and, in the end, distorted much of his mentor's theological thinking. In particular, he distorted Augustine's concept of predestination and irresistible grace. Instead, he proclaimed that believers needed to satisfy God's righteous demands. His solution was that of penance, priestly absolution, as well as the doctrine of purgatory, where one could work off one's sins. Gregory's distortions of Augustine's thinking provided an impetus to the Protestant reformers' efforts to reclaim Augustine's thinking for the church.

In the seventh century, the power of the bishop of Rome further increased due to the invasion of Mohammed from Arabia. Beginning in 622, his troops swept over many of the centers of Christianity in North Africa and into all but the northern part of Spain. However, in 732 Charles Martel at the Battle of Tours defeated the Muslim forces, which effectively ended the first wave of Muslim expansion. The effect of the Islamic aggression served as a background to the Reformation movement. With Jerusalem, Antioch, Damascus, Alexander, and Carthage under Muslim rule, the British Isles, France, the Low Countries, and Italy emerged as the centers of Christianity. The power of the bishop of Rome continued to increase to the point where church councils simply ratified the policies of the papacy.

Church Architecture

With most people being illiterate during the Middle Ages, beginning during the twelfth century, the architecture of the sanctuaries began to serve as an expression of church doctrine. In the transition from Romanesque architecture, with its thick walls and small windows, to the soaring walls and large stained glass windows of the Gothic style, sanctuaries communicated through their physical structures the biblical story. In addition, due to the church's doctrine of transubstantiation, in which the bread and wine become the body and blood of Christ in the Eucharist, sanctuaries needed to be physically grand enough for such a sacramental miracle. By the fifteenth century, congregations began to urge their priests to teach them the Scriptures. They therefore built pulpits within the sanctuaries from which their priests could preach, teach, and express informal prayers. The "service of the Word" began to have greater prominence in the church's worship.

Theological Scholasticism and Thomas Aquinas

During the twelfth century, theological scholasticism first took root within the monasteries, then branched out into the cathedral schools, and by the early thirteenth century had flowered within the universities. Thomas Aquinas (1224–1274) was one of the best-known proponents of such scholasticism. Born in the small town of Aquino, lying halfway between Rome and Naples, Thomas was one of seven sons of Landulf, the count of Aquino. His parents had intended that he enter the priesthood, where he potentially could hold a position of great power and influence. Toward that goal they sent him to study at the abbey of Monte Cassino when he only was five years old, and then on to the University of Naples when he was fourteen years of age. There his teachers first exposed him to the teachings of Aristotle. As the result of his vocational struggle, he joined the Dominican order in 1243. His family was horrified at the life that he had chosen, which included begging for provisions. In response, his brothers kidnapped him and locked him in a room for the night with a prostitute. They reasoned that he could not maintain his vows of celibacy against the sexual advances of the young woman. However, he remained celebate by using a hot poker from the fire to hold off her advances. Finally, drawing the sign of the cross on the wall with the poker, he fell to the floor begging God to grant him the gift of constant virginity. From that point onward, recognizing his strong sexual urges, he avoided the company of young women whenever possible.

During his early years in the monastery, many of those who knew Thomas Aquinas could not recognize in the large and quiet student the genius that lay within him. Some of his fellow students even began referring to him as "the dumb ox." However, as he began to assert himself in conversations, his superiors soon recognized his brilliance. They therefore sent him to the University of Cologne for undergraduate studies under Albertus Magnus, and then to Paris for advanced studies. In 1248, he returned to Cologne to teach as a subordinate of his mentor Magnus. After several years, the faculty "masters" admitted him to a teaching position at the University of Paris. During the next twenty-seven years, he continued teaching at Paris, as well as at Naples. In 1274, at barely fifty years of age, Thomas Aquinas died as the result of a stroke while staying at a Cistercian monastery on his way to the Council of Lyons. Only three years following his death, the archbishop of Paris, Stephen Tempier, banned his books, claiming that they were heretical. The archbishop of Canterbury followed suit. Yet, in time the church recognized the brilliance of his writings. When the church canonized him as a saint in 1323, Pope John XXII referred to the night when he defended his virginity against the sexual advances of a prostitute as the miracle needed for his sainthood. The second miracle was that, shortly before his death, a boat caught herring for him to eat, though herring were not normally found in that time and place.

Thomas Aquinas' Theological Contributions

Thomas Aquinas had not completed his lifelong great theological work, *Summa Theologiae*, at the time of his death. Nevertheless, his theological thinking has influenced theological education in the Roman Catholic Church to this day. His training in Aristotelian and Neo-Platonic philosophy, as well as in Islamic writers, greatly influenced his thinking. For Aquinas, God is sovereign and therefore created the world out of God's own goodness. His understanding of God's providence further affected all of this other theological thinking, especially his affirmation of "double predestination," that is, God having elected some persons to eternal life while having condemned others to eternal punishment. Further, for Aquinas, such predestination does not preclude one from the freedom of making choices for good or evil in this life. Those who were truly evil and not among the elect went straight to hell at death. However, those who were among the elect could cooperate with God's grace through doing benevolent works. Such acts of penance might add a mite to the abundance of merits that the saints had created. Yet, at death, even for the elect, their sins far exceeded their earned merits. The elect therefore went at death to purgatory. In purgatory, they could work off any remaining sins. The doctrine of purgatory goes back to Pope Gregory the Great (590–604), who first proposed the concepts of penance and purgatory.

In his understanding of the Eucharist, Aquinas taught the doctrine of transubstantiation. He based his understanding of what happens during the Eucharist on Platonic philosophical thought. In that philosophical system, Plato (427–348 BCE) taught that, just as all trees are different from one another, all trees likewise have something in common. Therefore, we can look at a pine tree or an oak tree or a maple tree, and call all of them trees. That is due to there being a "form" of a tree or an "ideal" tree that exists. We cannot see the ideal tree because it is beyond our world and beyond our own perceptions of time and space. Individual trees therefore all are in separately connected to this ideal or form of a tree. Christian Platonists in turn believed that God had developed such universal forms in heaven. From such universal forms in heaven, God had created all things. Therefore, when a priest repeated the words of consecration over the Eucharistic elements, God caused a miracle to happen. There was a transfer, or "transference of inner substance," from the ideal bread in heaven to the particular bread used in the worship celebration. The particular bread and the wine continued to look like normal bread and wine. Yet in reality, God had transformed them into being Christ's body and blood. Although the consecrated bread and wine did not look any different prior to being consecrated, for the believer that was not important. What mattered to the believer was that the universal form had given identity to the particular Eucharistic elements. In addition, because Christ at the Last Supper had held up the bread and said, "This is my body," the bread alone sufficiently contained all of Christ—his body and his blood. One therefore did not need to receive both the bread and the wine in order to receive fully the grace manifested in the eucharistic celebration. Not needing to receive the wine, many laypersons therefore chose to receive only the bread. By the twelfth century, receiving the bread alone had become the standard practice, lest one spill the wine.

Aquinas taught that since the church is one, when one suffers, we all suffer, and when one rejoices, we all rejoice. Therefore, as those in the church in heaven are inseparably connected with those in the church on earth, people could pray for those family and friends who were suffering in purgatory. Finally, as the pope was the head of the church, subjection to the pope was essential for salvation.

Further, Aquinas taught that although God might act in the universe as the "prime mover," God was not responsible for the "free will" choices that humans made in their lives. Further, his writings on sexuality today are relevant in the Roman Catholic Church's opposition to birth control and abortion. Finally, he formulated the basic tenants of "just war" versus "unjust war." His teachings would serve as a foundational writing for the later deliberations resulting in the Peace of Westphalia ending the Thirty Years War.

For Protestants, Thomas Aquinas' greatest contribution was his advocacy of reason as one means in the search for truth. Therefore, science and medicine are a proper means of understanding God's creation. His thinking was an advancement in Roman Catholic theology for that time. His writings in time would provide the fodder for Reformation thinkers and especially John Calvin.

Purgatory and Its Effects on Reformation Thinking

Popular belief in purgatory quickly grew during the rampage of the Black Death from 1348 to 1349. Particularly in the Western church, an entire institution of chantry priests developed to say Mass for the dead. Families could purchase a month's supply of Masses for the souls of their deceased loved ones. Yet, there remained skepticism that at death the truly evil went to hell, the saintly went to heaven, and the rest went to purgatory. Such skepticism led to the popular belief that those persons who died a "bad death" were condemned to wander aimlessly on the earth as a ghost, or as a spirit possessing a living human being. The church responded in declaring that demons, not the dead, could possess people. The Protestant movement sought to explain what happened to the soul between the immediate judgment at death and the second coming of Christ. Many leaders, including Tyndale and Luther, began to affirm the doctrine of "soul sleep," in which after death the soul would sleep until the Last Judgment. Such a belief filled the vacuum created by the Catholic Church's doctrine of purgatory. Still others, including Melanchthon, believed in the existence of ghosts. Most mainline reformers drew upon Augustine's wisdom that such ghosts actually were demons inhabiting peoples' bodies. They therefore encouraged congregations to affirm the helpful personal nature of angels as God's agents in the world. In such a manner, mainline reformers could replace the cult of the saints with a biblically sanctioned motif, and allowed art that depicted angels to remain within the sanctuaries.

Mysticism

Like the Mass, shrines were places where people could find spiritual comfort and renewal. People thought that when a saint entered heaven without having to undergo purgatory, that saint kept a spiritual connection with an earthly setting. Such a connection rendered the physical setting as sacred, and the church therefore built shrines in the saint's honor. For example, the cult of Mary taught that the Virgin Mary ascended to heaven without the experience of death. Her appearance to persons in certain places rendered those places as sacred. Later, the cult of Saint Ann, the mother of Mary, would have a special role in Martin Luther's life, as she was the patron saint of miners.

The devotion of the Order of Saint Bridget of Sweden, founded in the fourteenth century, instituted a systematic means of spiritual renewal. Using five beads, the ancestor of the Rosary, worshippers could recall aspects of Christ's passion. During this worship experience, worshippers recalled a thirty-three-word poem, with each bead recalling a particular phrase in the poem. In addition, worshippers prayed the Lord's Prayer fifteen times and the Hail Mary fifteen times. Over the course of a year, daily worship using the Rosary was to take off 5,475 years of purgatory.

Changes in the Educational System

During the Middle Ages, the Roman Catholic Church provided the foundation for education. The monasteries, as sanctuaries for education amidst the turbulent times, copied manuscripts and commentaries, passing along their knowledge on to a new generation of believers.

The cathedrals and monasteries provided the first schools. They focused on training students to be logical thinkers. Their curriculum centered on the seven liberal arts: Latin grammar, rhetoric, logic, arithmetic, geometry, music, and astronomy. With wealthy landowners financially endowing priests to say Mass for their family's deceased members, these chantry priests frequently served as the faculty in these first schools. The few students who excelled in their education were able to attend university.

The wealthy "bourgeois" wanted to send their sons off to the university towns so that they might receive the advanced training necessary for the practice of the professions of law, theology, and medicine. Therefore, around the year 1000, corporations began to charter universities and employ priests and monks for their faculty. Included in these new universities were those of Oxford (c. 1200), Paris (c. 1200), Bologna (c. 1200), Cambridge (c. 1209), and Naples (c. 1224). Their faculties were open to new ideas that challenged the traditional wisdom of the church. In addition, the Crusaders had returned, telling of a different religion, Islam, which challenged Christian teachings.

With the exemption of training in law and medicine, the curriculum focused on training in theology and church polity. Students flocked from all over Europe to attend these schools. Oxford and Paris were renowned for theology, Bologna for church and civil law, and Salerno for its medical education. The teaching methodology primarily was through lectures, as well as debates among students. As Latin was the universal language of scholarship, students from many different countries were among the student body.

Beginning in the 1400s, the new humanist educational system, with its increasing stress on the humanities, seemed to be effective in preparing students to play an active role in society. The humanist educational process began to seek to find answers for present challenges in the successes of the past—particularly in ancient Roman society. In northern Europe, Christians likewise began to look to early Christianity as the model for church transformation. The church, in turn, appointed many humanists as bishops, cardinals, and occasionally as pope. By the sixteenth century, the humanist movement was spreading throughout Europe.

Likewise, beginning in the early sixteenth century, the demand for administrators trained as lawyers began to increase. Every major city therefore began establishing "collegiums." Stricter educational standards were developed; new buildings had a staff of three to five "masters." The sons of the bourgeois and rentiers entered these schools as early as five years of age, learning Latin and Greek well enough to enter the study of law in their late teens. They stressed the liberal arts, including the disciplines of Latin, Greek, poetry, rhetoric, and philosophy. The schools were tuition free and open to all persons within the city. However, primarily the local elite were able to attend these schools, since many of the children within the lower social classes needed to work to help financially support their families. Graduates of these collegiums went on to Paris, Orleans, Toulouse, Valence, or Borges to study for the three professional disciplines. They married daughters of other educated rentiers, and moved away from their native cities. Many of these rentiers would become the tinder that would bring about the revolutions of Early Modern Europe.

Paper, the Printing Press, and the Transformation of Educational Methodology

The Revolutionary Effects of the Invention of the Printing Press

Two inventions enabled the mass communication of ideas and the development of political and religious movements. The Chinese had invented writing paper, manufactured from cloth rags. Such writing paper became standard in the thirteenth century, replacing reed-based papyrus or animal skins. By the end of the fourteenth century, Europe out-produced the Islamic world in the production of writing paper.

Secondly, the invention of the printing press was the most important technical invention that spurred on the Reformation and the Renaissance. The printing press was the result of technological collaboration between Johann Gutenberg, a goldsmith, who developed casting methods for type, Peter Schoffer, a copyist, who designed and set the printed text, and Johann Fust, who provided the financial capital for the venture. Jointly, they printed a Latin Bible in 1456, and an edition of the Psalms, drawing upon the much earlier Eastern invention of the woodcut and paper. By 1500, printing presses throughout Europe had printed between 6,000,000 to 15,000,000 books in 40,000 editions—more books than had been printed since the fall of the Roman Empire. In England alone, in the sixteenth century, 150,000,000 books were printed for a population of less than 80,000,000 people. Soon the printed book became the standard means of political, literary, and legal communication throughout Europe. Over time, the cost of books decreased, with a pamphlet in 1530 selling for the same price as a loaf of bread, and a copy of the New Testament selling for about the same as a laborer's daily wage.

A printing practice that seems to have delved into the macabre was that of "anthropodermic bibiopegy"—the binding of books with human skin. The practice goes back into the sixteenth century, and lasted to the early nineteenth century. The printer might bind an executed criminal's confession to his crime in a portion of his skin, or a person might specify that, following his death, a portion of his skin be the binding of a book as a family keepsake.[5] An article by the Catholic News Service (USCCB) reported on the auction of a seventeenth-century book that told of the 1605 Gunpowder Plot against the Protestant King James I, in which the investigators implicated certain Jesuit leaders. The book was titled, *A True and Perfect Relation of the Whole Proceedings Against the Late and Most Barbarous Traitors Garnet, a Jesuit and His Confederates*. The King's own bookbinder bound the book in a portion of the skin taken from the body of the perpetrators' Catholic confessor. After the court had convicted him of treason, on May 3, 1606, they hung Father Henry Garnet until he was almost dead, and then proceeded to have him "drawn and quartered" outside of St. Paul Cathedral in London. Father Garnet, the leader of the English Jesuits, was not directly involved in the plot, and had counseled against it. However, he was convicted because he had foreknowledge of the traitorous plot and did not warn government officials.[6]

The Printing Press Transforms Educational Methodology

The printing press likewise revolutionized the educational process. Prior to the invention of the printing press in the 1450s, students owned few books. They therefore spent hours copying phrase by phrase the lectures given by their teachers. Likewise, the question-and-answer format was a frequent educational methodology. Later, debating became an educational format. With the invention of the printing press, the availability of books transformed educational methodology. One cannot overestimate the magnitude of the effects of the printing press. With manuscripts, the medieval reader frequently added their own corrections or remarks in the wide margins. Monks copying manuscripts often would insert into the manuscript's body the corrections and the remarks that readers had written. However, printing presses copied books according to the original manuscript without any such editorial corrections. For the first hundred years, Erasmus, Luther,

   5. Madrigal, "It Was Once Common to Bind Books With Human Skin."
   6. Caldwell, "Book Bound in Skin of Executed Jesuits at Auction in England."

and Machiavelli used manuscripts and books for the distribution of their writings. Further, due to popular resistance to the printed book, many early printers used scribes to illuminate printed books to imitate the appearance of manuscripts. Some scholars even suggested that the printed page was only a passing fad that would last, at the most, a couple hundred years! The earliest dated book that has survived to this day is a Latin edition of the Psalter, printed in Mainz in 1457.

The urban centers were the cauldrons of modern individualism. Yet, concurrently, they saw themselves as religious communities responsible for the moral and social welfare of their inhabitants. The leaders of the Reformation and the Renaissance would find common ground in their mutual concern for the social welfare of society. Calvin, Zwingli, and Melanchthon were supportive of the new learning, even more so than was Martin Luther. However, all of them realized that the importance of education grew out of his doctrine of the "priesthood of all believers." That is, every person, even the lowest peasant, should be educated to be able to understand the most moving sermon in the loftiest cathedral. Through the printed word, their teachings would reach to the uttermost parts of the world.

2

Forerunners of the Protestant Reformation

Augustine of Hippo

THE SEMINAL IDEAS THAT flowered into the Protestant Reformation began centuries before in the teachings of Augustine, bishop of Hippo (354–430). Augustine was born in Thageste, in North Africa (now Souk-Ahras, Algeria), a small community situated on the crossroads leading to seemingly more important places. Augustine grew up as the son of a minor Roman official, Patrick, who was a pagan, and who owned a few acres of land and a couple of slave girls. His mother, Monica, was a devoted Christian. From his early years, Augustine felt alienated from his father, but was extremely close to his mother. Tragically, while Augustine was yet a troubled teenager, his father died. Augustine also had a brother and a sister, but we do not know his siblings' birth order. His early schooling was at Thageste, where his teacher used the cane on Augustine too frequently. He went on to study at the nearby Madaura community school. Soon realizing that Augustine possessed extraordinary academic gifts, a wealthy neighbor, Romanianus, financially enabled him to study in Carthage. A sensitive and introspective young man, Augustine would look back on his early education with disappointment. Instead, he educated himself through reading many of the great authors in Latin and Greek.

While studying in Carthage, to the horror of his mother, he developed a sexually intimate relationship with a young woman from a lower social class. She would become pregnant and give birth to their child. Augustine named his son Adeodatus, which means "given by God." Like Augustine, the boy was very intelligent, but sadly died when he was seventeen years of age. Augustine lived faithfully with the young woman for thirteen years.

Ultimately, his mother persuaded him that continuing the relationship would hinder his career advancement. He therefore ended the relationship.

In preparing for a career in law or public service, Augustine studied rhetoric, in particular the writings of Cicero, particularly his *Hortensius*. In his search for his own faith, Augustine became a follower of Manichaeism, a philosophy that rationally sought to explain good and evil. He found that the rational, sophisticated-seeming nature of the philosophy was attractive compared to the inelegant, primitive, and frequently violent writings in the Bible. Yet Manichaeism did not answer his major life's question: Since God is good, why then is there evil in the world? In his search for truth for his life, he moved to Milan and became a follower of Neo-Platonism, particularly the teachings of Plotinus. Through his studies, he came to understand that evil is not a manifestation of a spiritual being, but rather a movement away from God's goodness. Throughout his studies, he struggled to understand how he could experience a higher spiritual relationship with God, given his constant and overpowering sexual urges.

Encouraged by his mother, he traveled to hear Bishop Ambrose preach. There he found in Ambrose's allegorical interpretations of the Scriptures a solution to his problems with the seeming primitiveness of the Bible. A searcher for truth, he also began to study the writings of Plotinus, as interpreted by Plotinus's pupil and biographer, Porphyry. Porphyry taught that one could gain happiness in life only by following the ancient Delphi commandment, "Know thyself." Porphyry wrote, "Our end is to attain the contemplation of Being"; "He who knows God has God present to him"; and "He who does not know is absent from God who is everywhere present."[1] Not surprisingly, Augustine's own writing of his *Confessions* echoed Porphyry's teachings. In July 386, in Milan, while suffering from asthma, he had a conversion experience in the garden of the home. There he seemed to hear a child's voice telling him to read the Scriptures. He opened the Bible to see what passage he first would see. His eyes first fell upon Romans 13:13–14, where he read Paul's words to put on Christ in contrast to sexual wantonness. In that moment, Augustine discovered the compass for his life. Eight months later, on Easter 387, Ambrose baptized Augustine into the Christian faith. During the same service, Ambrose further baptized Augustine's son, Adeodatus, and his close friend Alypius, an attorney. Alypius later would become the bishop of Thagaste.

---

1. Chadwick, *Augustine*, 21.

Augustine's conversion had not come suddenly. Instead, perhaps like that of Apostle Paul, his conversion was the result of many months of spiritual anguish. Augustine was thirty-three years old at the time. With his newfound compass for his life, he resigned from his teaching position in rhetoric and moved to North Africa with his mother in order to enter the reflective life of a monk. Along the way, his mother suddenly died. He was so grief-stricken that he retreated to Rome for several months. Finally, Augustine arrived in Tiagaste in North Africa, where he gave away all his personal possessions to the poor, intent with several friends to live a life of mystic contemplation. He established a lay community that met daily for contemplative prayer and the recitation of the Psalter. However, instead of the life of a monk, God had other plans in store for Augustine. In 391, he visited a friend in the small town of Hippo. While there, they attended worship. The bishop, Valerius, recognized him and persuaded him to be ordained as the presbyter of the small Christian congregation there. As a compromise to Augustine's monastic leanings, the bishop agreed for him to build a monastery on the church grounds. Four years later, he was ordained the coadjutor bishop of Hippo. In 396, upon Valerius' death, he became the bishop of Hippo.

Augustine would become the most influential theologian of the Latin-speaking church. Although he wrote against the teachings of Manichaeism and Neo-Platonism, perhaps his most important contributions were against the Pelagians. Pelagius was a British monk who taught that since one has freedom of will, one can by one's own efforts overcome sin's corrupting influence. In contrast, Augustine taught that even though we have the freedom to choose between good and evil, even our best and most selfless choices always contain a taint of sin. That taint of sin is the result of humanity's "fall" in the Garden of Eden. Feeling that only God could bridge the gap between God's holiness and our innate sinfulness, Augustine later developed the doctrines of predestination and irresistible grace, Augustine further developed the understanding of God as "three persons in one substance," one of the theological affirmations later found in the Nicene Creed. Two of his major writings were the thirteen-volume *Confessions*, an autobiography addressed as a prayer to God, and the twenty-two volume *City of God*, which he wrote in 410 to console Christians following the Visigoths sacking of Rome. Due to his belief that God is the Lord of heaven and earth, he spoke out against capital punishment and slavery. He further called for tolerance and reconciliation within the church. Not one to shun the secular disciplines, Augustine heartily approved of scientific inquiry. His extensive library included a number of medical textbooks.

According to Douglas Ottati, Roman Catholics emphasize Augustine's doctrine of the church, as well as his arguments against the Donatists. In particular, Roman Catholics emphasize that "(1) sanctification and a changed life is a condition for justification or forgiveness; (2) genuine faith is faith in the authoritative teaching of the Catholic Church; and (3) saving grace is available only in the sacraments of the true (and visible) Roman Catholic Church."[2]

In contrasting Protestants to Roman Catholics, Ottati writes further:

> An Augustinian Protestant is one whose understanding of the Bible and the life of faith affirms and even radicalizes Augustine's broad theology of grace. This describes the emphasis of Luther and Calvin: persons are good and limited creatures, radically corrupted by sin, but nevertheless forgiven, turned, and enabled by grace alone to respond faithfully to God and others.[3]

In addition, Ottati clarifies the difference between Luther and Calvin in their understandings of the role of grace in one's life:

> Lutherans often emphasize justification and grace as free forgiveness; Reformed communities agree, but they also emphasize a changed way of life. That is, they point to both reconciliation and renewal. In this they follow John Calvin, who spoke of 'a double grace,' or both justification—being pardoned by Christ's blamelessness—and sanctification—being renewed by Christ's spirit— and who emphasized the latter so much that he treated it before the former in his *Institutes*.[4]

Augustine died in 430, as the Vandals were at the gates of Hippo. As he lay dying, his last thoughts were of his mentor, Plotinus. In the end, Augustine would become, through various interpretations of his thought, the most influential theologian of the Western church, both Protestant and Catholic.

---

2. Ottati, *Theology for Liberal Protestants*, 5.
3. Ibid., 13.
4. Ibid., 13–14.

Forerunners of the Protestant Reformation

The Post-Augustinian Church Faces New Challenges

Justo Gonzalez has written:

> Jerome died in 420, Theodore in 428, Augustine in 430. Not only were the great interpreters of Scripture dying, but also the ancient world. Ten years before the death of Jerome, Rome was sacked by the Goths. Soon the entire western portion of the Roman Empire would be divided among several Germanic kingdoms. In the centuries that ensured, when civil disorder, foreign invasions, and economic chaos were common occurrences, most of the science and wisdom salvaged from antiquity took refuge in the church and its institutions, particularly the monasteries. As a result, for centuries, the Bible was read through monastic eyes.[5]

Understandably, the monks interpreted the Scriptures as God's call for monastic renunciation of the devil, the flesh, and worldly sins. During the spiritual reign of Pope Gregory the Great, and throughout the following five centuries, there was little theological debate in comparison with that during the time of Origen and Augustine. The church interpreted Scripture allegorically, instead of seeking to understand the plain meaning of the text.

With the arrival of the twelfth century, and the development of the cathedral schools and later universities, new approaches began to develop in the interpretation of Scripture. Among these new approaches was an effort to understand the Scriptures as a source of knowledge and theological insight. A number of scholars, in addition to their teaching responsibilities, wrote commentaries on portions of Scripture. They based their commentaries on the Latin Vulgate translation of the Bible, as theological students did not learn Hebrew and Greek as a part of their curriculum.

Over the centuries, the church had become dysfunctional due to inept leadership, poor theological training, and increasing corruption. Finally, the increasingly dysfunctional state of the church during the fourteenth and fifteenth centuries would seek to correct itself through various reformation movements. In one of those efforts, referred to as the Conciliar Movement, the bishops attempted to end the schism of two different popes each claiming papal authority, the practices of purchasing church offices, and nepotism. In the first instance, that of two popes, the nations of Europe had divided their loyalty between the differing papacies. One papacy was located in Avignon, France, and the other in Rome. Each of the two popes

---

5. Gonzalez, "How the Bible Has Been Interpreted in Christian Tradition," 95–96.

refused to seek a positive resolution to the schism. The Roman cardinals, in an effort toward reconciliation, broke with their own papacy in Rome, and began negotiations with the French cardinals owing alliance to the papacy at Avignon. As a result, they called a joint council to gather at Pisa in 1409, in an effort to end the Great Schism. However, true to the dysfunctional nature of the system, both of the popes refused to participate in the council meeting. Each pope then withdrew to his own fortified stronghold. At Pisa, the council determined that both popes were unworthy and both were deposed. The council then acted to elect Alexander V as the new pope, to replace both of the deposed popes. Unfortunately, less than a year after the cardinals elected him pope, he died. The cardinals then elected John XXIII to be his successor.[6] With the Hundred Years War going on at the time, John XXIII sought refuge with Sigismund, the king of Hungary, and later the Holy Roman Emperor. John XXIII received refuge on the condition that he would agree to a new council at Constance in 1414. At that council meeting, surprised by the vote for his resignation, John XXIII fled. However, later the council captured him, forced him to resign, and imprisoned him for the rest of his life. The council then elected Martin V as the new successor to John XXIII. In addition to working to end the schism, the council at Constance further attempted to rid the church of heretics. In doing so, they condemned John Huss to death. We will read more about John Huss further in this section.

Another council followed at Pavia in 1423. However, due to an outbreak of the bubonic plague, attendance was very low. In 1430, the next council gathered, Martin V suddenly died, at which point the council elected Eugene IV as pope. Due to the rapid turnover of popes, the power of the councils rivaled that of the pope. Some members of the council even expressed hope for a joint episcopacy, with the pope having limited powers. However, with the threat of the Turkish invasion of Constantine, Eugene IV used the anxious atmosphere in the council to divide it. As a result, the Conciliar Movement, which promised great reform, in the end left the church divided into two councils with one pope. Under the leadership of Eugene IV's successor, Felix V, the church acknowledged papal supremacy, and the efforts at governance reform seemed lost.

---

6. Note that there was a John XXIII in the fifteenth century and a Pope John XXIII in the twentieth century. This duplication of names has been due to the church at Rome today not recognizing as legitimate any previous popes that did not reside in Rome.

Forerunners of the Protestant Reformation

Peter Abelard

Despite the failure of the efforts at a reformation of the church's governance, there were efforts to reform the church's theology and manner of faith expression. Yet the church was slow to change. In 1100, Peter Abelard, a Frenchman, sought to include human reason as one of the means of understanding the meanings of the Scriptures. He was condemned as a heretic. Although the church court spared his life, they forced him to watch the burning of his books. His primary theological opponent was Bernard of Clairvaux, a French Abbot (1090–1153) who taught that Christians should willingly accept the church's teachings without question. Peter Abelard died in one of the Cluny monasteries.

Thomas Bradwardine

An Englishman, Thomas Bradwardine, was an eminent Catholic theologian and teacher at Oxford. Bradwardine in his study of Augustinian theology came to an understanding of the doctrine of predestination as a positive affirmation of God's benevolent grace unto us. Accordingly, he felt that with the knowledge that we freely have received salvation, we could enjoy our personal relationship with God. Despite his seemingly radical theological assertions, Thomas Bradwardine held the respect of his peers and the pope. He died in 1349 serving as the archbishop of Canterbury.

John Wycliffe

Another Englishman, John Wycliffe, was born in Yorkshire in 1330. Wycliffe lived during the Avignon papacy and died just prior to the Great Schism. He studied at Balliot College, Oxford, where the faculty and students quickly recognized his intelligence. Although most scholars consider Wycliffe to have had no equal theologians in his day, aspects of his theological system remained feudal in its concepts. As with the later reformers, Augustine's theology greatly influenced Wycliffe's own thinking.

By 1376, Wycliffe was speaking out against the church's wealth and influence in political life. In 1377, in his lecture "On Civil Lordship," he asserted that God is the great feudal overlord who appoints persons to civil and ecclesiastical responsibilities. As such, all earthly subjects are to manifest faithful stewardship of one's possessions. When anyone therefore fails to manifest such faithful stewardship, clergy or layperson, those persons should lose their positions of authority. Further, Wycliffe taught that the Scriptures are the only reliable standard for the guiding one in the Christian lifestyle. Most upsetting to the papacy was his assertion that the head of the Church is Jesus Christ, not the pope. Wycliffe went so far as to write that the pope might not be a member of the elect. He did not object to the pope governing the church, but asserted that the Scriptures are to have final authority in matters of faith. Understandably, his teaching threatened the authority of the papacy. The pope in turn sought five times to have Wycliffe arrested. Nevertheless, he avoided arrest due to his local popularity.

Between 1382 and 1384, John Wycliffe oversaw the translation of the Scriptures from the Latin Vulgate. He perhaps even had a hand in the translation of the New Testament. In 1379, Wycliffe made a fatal mistake in attacking the doctrine of transubstantiation, and proposed an alternative understanding of the Eucharist. As a result, a number of his followers stopped supporting his cause. At the same time, the Peasants Revolt in 1381 strengthened the more conservative elements within the church. With the shift of some of his local support and the theological swing in the church, the papacy was able to prohibit Wycliffe from teaching at Oxford. Subsequently appointed to serve in a pastorate at Lutterworth, he died of a stroke on the last day of 1384. As he officially remained in communion with the church, the church buried him on consecrated ground in the church cemetery. However, in an attempt to suppress dissent within the church, on May 4, 1415, the Council of Constance condemned Wycliffe of heresy, then disinterred and burned his remains. To keep his followers from collecting unconsumed bits of his bones as relics, they threw his ashes into the Swift River.

The Lollard Movement

Yet, even the disposal of his earthly physical remains could not consume Wycliffe's teachings. Many of Wycliffe's followers were noblemen and gentry who favored any doctrine that might lead to the church losing control of its massive land holdings. These and other followers soon claimed the name of the "Lollards," meaning "mumblers." They rejected transubstantiation, praying for the dead, pastors holding civil offices, images within the churches, pilgrimages to shrines, and clergy celibacy. In 1401, Henry IV, in an effort to gain approval from the pope, began persecuting and burning Lollards at the stake. However, Henry IV did not extend his persecution to the leaders of the movement. His son Henry V, however, in 1417 executed Sir John Oldcastle, Lord of Cobham, a movement leader. Wycliffe's teaching would have its greatest lasting influence among the Christians in Bohemia. By a turn of God's providence, with the marriage of the English King Richard III to Anna, a Bohemian princess, and Richard's ascension to the throne in 1483, the new political alliance allowed a number of Bohemian students to study at Oxford. In their studies, they discovered Wycliffe's ideas. In 1485, Richard III died at the Battle of Bosworth Field, just two years into his reign. The victor, the future Henry VII, in killing Richard III, thereupon ushered in the Tudor family's royal reign. The Tudor ascension to the throne, likewise, became a benchmark in the emergence of Early Modern Europe.

John Huss

Bohemia, now Czechoslovakia, was the birthplace of the reformer John Huss. Born in about 1373 from peasant parents in Husinecz, he claimed the last name of Huss. Studies at the University of Prague earned him a Bachelor of Theology in 1394 and a Master of Arts in 1396. Huss thereupon was ordained a priest in 1401, and a year later was appointed as the rector of the University of Prague. A popular and renowned preacher, Huss likewise served as the priest of the Bethlehem Chapel in Prague. John Huss appreciated Wycliffe's teachings, particularly his understanding of the doctrine of election. However, Huss did not adopt many of Wycliffe's more extreme teachings, such as that of consubstantiation. At the same time, some of his fellow faculty members considered Huss and some of his colleagues to be too liberal for their tastes. They therefore left their teaching positions at Prague and founded a new university at Leipzig.

Politically, Huss was very nationalistic, and through his church reforms he sought to limit Germany's power over his fellow Slavic people. Theologically, he proposed that priests conduct the worship liturgy in the language of the people, and that laypeople receive the wine during the celebration of the Lord's Supper. Troubled by reports of Huss's actions, in 1410 Pope Martin V summoned Huss to travel to Rome to answer for his actions. Huss refused to go to Rome, fearing for his life. The Pope in 1411 responded to Huss' refusal to travel to Rome by excommunicating him. Huss then openly defied Pope Martin V in stating that the Bible is supreme for life and practice—not the pope. Moreover, Huss stated, if the pope does not obey the Bible, the pope is not a legitimate pope. Once again, in an effort to control his renegade priest, the pope excommunicated Huss for heresy. For his safety, Huss withdrew from Prague into the countryside and continued to write.

Pope Martin V realized that there was an increasing religious dissent within the church. He therefore called the Council at Constance to help resolve these differences. In a sign of support, the Holy Roman Emperor Sigismund invited Huss to attend the meeting, and granted him a safe conduct pass. However, when Huss arrived, the church leadership refused to listen to his views and ordered him to recant. When he refused, they arrested and imprisoned him. The emperor at first had supported Huss in his theological assertions. However, when he saw that the Bohemian populace increasingly was not supportive of Huss's theology, he withdrew his pledge of safe passage back to Bohemia. While in prison, Huss learned that on May 4 the council members had disinterred and burned Wycliffe's body. He therefore knew that he had little chance of living.

On June 5, 1415, Huss once again appeared before the council, where he definitely declared, "I appeal to Jesus Christ, the only judge who is almighty and completely just. In his hands, I place my cause, since he will judge each, not on the basis of false witnesses and erring councils but of truth and justice." The following day they took him to the cathedral, tore his priestly garments from his body, and shaved his head. In mocking him, they placed a paper crown decorated with drawings of devils on his head. On his way to the stake, they led him past a flaming pyre where others were burning his books. They tied him to the stake, where once again he defiantly refused to recant his views. Instead, he prayed aloud, "Lord Jesus, it is for Thee that I patiently endure this cruel death. I pray Thee to have mercy on my enemies."[7] As the flames consumed Huss's body, bystanders reported hearing him reciting from the Psalms.

A few days later, they likewise burned his colleague, Jerome of Prague, who had joined Huss at the council. As they had done with Wycliffe's ashes, the executioners likewise gathered Huss's ashes and threw them into a lake to erase all evidence of their lives. However, some brave Czech followers gathered bits of the soil from where Huss had burned to death. They then established themselves as the Hussite Church in Bohemia, a new church independent of Rome. Devoted to the celebration of the Mass, they initiated frequent celebrations, as well as allowed children to receive the elements.

---

7. Gonzalez, *Story of Christianity*, 1:350–51.

Because of their emphasis on the Eucharist celebration, the eucharistic chalice became a symbol of their movement. In turn, a Hussite general named Jan Zizka ("One-Eyed John") led the Bohemians in a revolt. In the end, the church made some minor concessions, including permitting the giving of the wine to the laity during the Eucharist. Otherwise, however, no significant changes took place. The established church feared the Hussite movement for generations. We will hear more about the Hussite movement when we read the story of the reformer Martin Luther.

The Beginnings of the Moravian Movement

Some of Wycliffe's followers in Moravia did not accept the peace terms between the church and the Hussite movement. Faithful in their worship and service, despite great persecution, their numbers grew rapidly over the years. A religious nobleman, Count Zinzendorf, offered them sanctuary on his estate in Saxony. This movement would evolve into the religious branch of Protestantism known as the Moravian Brethren, another Calvinistic branch on the tree of the Christian faith. Moravian teachings would greatly influence the theological teachings of John Wesley, the father of Methodism.

Johannes Geiler von Kaysersberg

Born March 16, 1445, in Schaffhausen, Switzerland, Johannes Geiler von Kaysersberg and his family moved a few months after his birth to Ammerschweier in Upper Alsace. His father died in a hunting accident when Johannes Geiler was yet a child. His grandfather in the neighboring town of Kaysersberg undertook the responsibility of rearing him. At fifteen years of age he entered the University of Freiburg in Breisgau, later studying theology at Basel. In 1475, after completing his doctorate, he returned to Freiburg to teach theology. Yet, restless in an academic setting, he felt God's call to move from the university to the parish setting. After preaching a trial sermon at Wurzburg, the congregation enthusiastically invited him to remain as their minister. It seemed as if he would spend several years ministering to the congregation in Wurzburg. Yet, on his return to Basel to gather his books and other personal items, he stopped in the city of Strasbourg. Peter Schott heard of his presence and invited him to remain there as the minister of the Strasbourg Cathedral. Sensing God's call in the invitation from Strasbourg, he declined the invitation of the Wurzburg congregation.

He moved to Strasbourg for the next thirty-two years of his ministry. He was concerned for moral reform within the city. His preaching therefore stressed that, in God's justice, God gives God's grace to those persons who seek to live a moral life. After the death of Johannes Geiler in 1510, his moral reforms continued to be a vital force in Strasbourg. However, in time, the reforms began to decline. Yet his modest ethical reforms would lay the groundwork for the later Protestant Reformation movement at Strasbourg.

Johannes von Staupitz

For Protestants, the careers of Johannes von Staupitz and Martin Luther intertwine. Born in 1460 or 1469, von Staupitz served as Luther's superior in the Augustinian order, and as Luther's predecessor as the professor of Bible at Wittenberg. Further, throughout Luther's career he would continue as Luther's advisor and friend. He was born in Motterwitz to a family of Swiss nobility. One of his childhood playmates was the future Frederick the Wise, the elector of Saxony. Taking his vows as a member of the Order of the Hermits of Saint Augustine in 1497, Johannes von Staupitz continued his theological studies at Tubingen. Completing a doctorate in 1500, he moved to Munich, where he served as the prior of the Augustine monastery. His contemplative life was interrupted by the insistence of his childhood playmate, Frederick the Wise, that he become the professor of Bible at Frederick the Wise's newly created University of Wittenberg. At the same time, he also assumed the position of vicar general of the Reformed Congregation of the Hermits of Saint Augustine.

As Luther's superior at the monastery, von Staupitz encouraged Luther to earn his doctorate, and to become the professor of Bible at Wittenberg. Further, von Staupitz influenced Luther toward an appreciation of Augustinian theology. Particularly, von Staupitz stressed Augustine's concept of a loving, personal, and gracious God—a God through whose unconditional election of sinners determines the scope and tone of our salvation. In time, assailed by church authorities for his relationship with Luther, von Staupitz feared for his life. In 1520, after twenty years as vicar general, he felt constrained to resign his position in order to become the advisor to the court of Salzburg. In 1522 he was consecrated an abbot. Von Staupitz died on December 28, 1524, loyal to Luther to the end. Following his death, in an effort to suppress his teachings, Pope Paul IV placed his books on the Index of Unapproved Writings.

FORERUNNERS OF THE PROTESTANT REFORMATION

Johann Reuchlin

Very early on, church leaders recognized an Italian, Johann Reuchlin, for his abilities in Latin, Greek, and Hebrew. They therefore sent him to the University of Paris, where he studied Greek, and he went on to receive his master's degree from Basel in 1477. Further studies continued at the Universities at Orleans and Poitiers. Appointed to serve as an aide to the count of Württemberg, Reuchlin was able to travel widely and pursue his scholarly interests. In 1506, Reuchlin published a Hebrew grammar and lexicon. His groundbreaking publication greatly improved the ability of theological students to study the Hebrew Bible. Although Johann Reuchlin disapproved of the emerging Reformation movement, his grandnephew, the reformer Philip Melanchthon, inherited his intellectual genius. We will read more about Melanchthon in connection with Martin Luther.

Desiderius Erasmus

Desiderius Erasmus was a leading humanist theologian at the time. The details of his birth are uncertain. We do know that he was born out of wedlock to a priest and a physician's daughter, in Rotterdam or Gouda in Holland, either in 1466 or 1469. Early in his childhood, Erasmus adopted many of the common values of the bourgeoisie population, notably tolerance, stability, and moderation. While attending the school of Deventer, Erasmus discovered his love of writing, and appreciated the spiritual piety within the Brethren of Common Life. The Brethren of Common Life was a reform movement that Gerhard Groote had founded in the Netherlands in the late fourteenth century. The Brethren sought to encourage people to center their lifestyle on daily devotional reading of the Bible, communal life, church attendance, ordered prayer, and self-examination. Most people in Germany or the Low Countries received their basic education at schools provided by the Brethren of Common Life. Erasmus, not having the financial means to pursue another profession, chose to enter the Augustinian monastery at Steyn. However, he soon discovered that his temperament was not congenial to that of the structured and solitary life of a monk. His superiors, likewise, recognized that fact. Therefore, when the bishop ordained him in 1492, he appointed Erasmus the secretary to the bishop of Cambrai. By 1495, Erasmus was a student in Paris. By 1498, he had obtained the Bachelor of Divinity degree. By 1499, he was traveling in England, where he became friends of John Colet and Thomas More. The three men soon discovered that they shared a mutual interest in the writings of Cicero, Socrates, and the Apostle Paul. Colet encouraged Erasmus to study Greek so that he might be able to read the New Testament in the original language. Afterward, Erasmus traveled extensively throughout Italy, taught Greek at Cambridge, as well as in the Netherlands. From 1521, he made his home in Basel, from where he published his Greek edition of the New Testament. However, when Basel embraced the Reformation movement, Erasmus moved to Freiburg. In 1536, while on a visit to Basel he died.

In his genius, Erasmus realized the importance of the printing press for the mass communication of ideas. Therefore, in 1516, he published the first printed Greek edition of the New Testament. He further would publish a Latin translation of the New Testament, as well as later works on the church fathers. Although Erasmus saw the errors in the Catholic Church, he chose to remain within it and to work for reform. For Erasmus, reform would come through the process of educating the church leadership in the original Christian sources. In that way, the church could return to its original purity. Erasmus had little interest in debating the theoretical issues regarding the sacraments, or the daily controversial religious issues. Instead, in remaining true to his training by the Brethren of Common Life, he was pragmatic in his approach to faith. He focused his teachings on Jesus' ethical teachings found in the Sermon on the Mount. Oddly enough, Erasmus later would end up in a conflict with his fellow Augustinian monk Martin Luther. Erasmus, however, refused to support the Catholic attacks upon the Protestants. To the very end, he called for tolerance, and for living out the ancient virtues of the Stoics and Platonists. Although few at the time followed his humanistic approach of mutual forbearance, centuries later, after the passions have subsided, Protestants and Catholics agree that all have much to learn from him.

3

The Reformation in Germany

Martin Luther

PETER MARSHALL DESCRIBES IT this way:

> It starts in a thunderstorm in the summer of 1505. On the road near Erfurt, in the Germany principality of Saxony, a young law student is caught in a downpour, and fears for his life amidst ferocious strikes of lightning. He prays to St. Anne, the mother of the Virgin Mary, offering a bargain: if she will spare his life, he will become a monk. A fortnight later, he bangs on the door of the Erfurt house of the reformed Augustinian friars, one of the strictest of all the religious orders.[1]

Martin Luther told this story about himself many decades later. It was his attempt to explain the unexplainable—how he had experienced the Holy Other in the midst of a thunderstorm, and how that experience had shaped his life. Apostle Paul met the risen Christ on the Road to Damascus. Young Moses realized that he was standing in God's presence before the burning bush. Prophet Isaiah experienced God's presence in the smoke-filled temple. Likewise, on the road from Mansfield to Erfurt, the twenty-one-year-old Martin Luther realized the presence of God amidst the terrible thunder, blinding lightening, and drenching downpour. God later would use Luther as tinder in order to set the world aflame with the spirit of spiritual reformation.

---

1. Marshall, *Reformation*, 11

The Early Years

Luther was born in Eisleben, Germany, in 1483, the year prior to the birth of another reformer, Huldrych Zwingli. As he was born on the feast of St. Martin of Tours, his parents named him Martin. He would be the eldest of seven children, with only one brother (Jacob or James) and three sisters surviving to adulthood. His other two brothers died in the 1505 plague. Luther's birth likewise occurred only a year after the printing of Ptolemy's second-century maps, which reshaped people's understanding of the world. Luther's father, Hans Luther, was of peasant origin, and never learned to read. Nevertheless, beginning work as a miner, he later became the partial owner of several foundries. Yet despite his father's professional success, young Martin's childhood was not a happy one. His parents were very severe with him. Luther's experiences in school, likewise, were very difficult. Due to the lack of books, and paper being very expensive, the teacher wrote the lessons on the blackboard, which the students copied on slates. Luther later painfully recounted how one teacher whipped him fifteen times in the same morning, for not for not knowing how to decline and conjugate the Latin nouns and verbs. Certainly, those difficult early childhood traumas left an imprint on Martin Luther's life, which later manifested themselves in his lifelong struggles with anxiety and periods of severe depression.

As Luther's father had great personal ambition for himself, he also felt great personal ambition for his son. When Martin was a child, his father moved his family to Mansfield, where Martin attended the Magdeburg school located next to the cathedral. He sang in the choir and possessed a beautiful tenor voice. Luther loved music, and once claimed that music was second only to theology in comforting one's soul. A year later, Luther attended the famous Latin school of St. George in Eisenach, where he spent four enjoyable years. Several extended family members and family friends lived within that community, with whom he frequently visited. In 1502, the St. George school granted him a Bachelor of Arts degree, placing thirteenth in a class of fifty-seven students. Continuing his studies at St. George, in 1505 they granted him the Master of Arts degree, placing second in a class of seventeen students. Hans Luther had struggled to send his son to the finest universities so that he might become a successful lawyer and a member of the rising middle class.

The Reformation in Germany

God Encounters Luther in a Thunderstorm

Yet, Luther's night in a violent thunderstorm and his encounter with God became the sole driving force in his life. Therefore, in defiance of his father, he sold all of his books, except Plautus and Virgil, and knocked on the wooden door of the monastery next to his St. George school. In April 1507, at twenty-two years of age, Martin Luther was ordained as an Augustinian monk. A month later, he administered his first Mass, with his proud Father and twenty-three relatives attending the service. Luther went on to study at the University of Erfurt where he earned a Master of Arts degree in 1505, followed by earning a Bachelor of Theology at Wittenberg in 1509. Finally, in 1512, he likewise earned a Doctor of Theology, and began lecturing on the Bible at Wittenberg. He briefly would be called back to teach at Erfurt, but after a year returned to Wittenberg. In his classes, he began lecturing on the Psalms. He wanted his students to hear the message of the Psalms anew, without the filter of the medieval commentaries. Therefore, Luther printed them without any commentary added. Although Wittenberg, the capitol of the Electoral Saxony, today is a small city, in 1513 it was a small town with only 356 houses, mostly built of mud with straw thatched roofs, and a new university. Luther, realizing the primitive sanitary conditions within the town, refused to drink the local water, considering it unsafe. Instead, he drank beer and wine, brewing his own beer at home.

Even though immersed in academia, Luther personally could not resolve his internal struggles. His spiritual roadblock was his image of God, for Luther envisioned God in the image of his demanding father and his abusive early teachers. He therefore felt he never could please such a demanding and abusive God! Overwhelming feelings of guilt returned, and they began to consume his every waking moment. In an effort to find peace for his wounded soul, Luther spent hours each day going to Confession. There, he would confess in detail every minor sin in order to feel absolution. Yet Luther could not find peace for his soul. Finally, his confessor was frustrated with hearing Luther drone over the minutest matters, and told him not to come back until he could confess some real sins worth hearing.

"The Righteousness of God"

Yet God did not leave Luther alone to face his fears in his search for meaning in his life. While meditating on Romans, Luther read the phrase "the righteousness of God" from Romans 1:17. As a light suddenly enables one to see all about a room, in reading Romans 1:17 Luther could spiritually see clearly for the first time in his life. He realized that he has been trying to do the impossible. Through biblical study, he realized that "the righteousness of God" was freely conveyed to him by God. It was not through his futile efforts to be righteous before a demanding and abusive God. From that point onward, Luther began to share his new insights with the larger Roman Catholic Church. He wrote, "I felt that I had been born anew and that the gates of heaven had been opened. The whole of Scripture had gained a new meaning. And from that point on the phrase 'the justice of God' no longer filled me with hatred, but rather became unspeakably sweet by virtue of a great love."[2]

Luther shared his insights concerning God's gift of grace. Yet, Luther was swimming upstream against centuries of the church's theology. Before long, Martin Luther and the pope faced off due to different understandings of God and the means of God's grace. The triggering event would be the sale of indulgences. According to the theological mindset of that era, the church believed that any wrong committed against another person required a personal restitution to the injured party. God likewise must demand restitution for wrongs committed against God. Even though one confessed one's sins to a priest, there remained sins needing atonement and acts of penitence. Those sins that remained when one had died needed atonement in purgatory. Only after one had completed such penance in purgatory could one proceed onward to heaven. In time, in order to increase the number of sales of indulgences, the pope arranged for people to be able to purchase indulgences or merits on behalf of the dead that could release them early from purgatory.

Salvation and Fund Raising

The particular indulgences that Luther objected to had economic and political consequences. Albert, as a member of the powerful Germanic House of Hohenzollern, already possessed two bishoprics and wished to purchase the influential archbishopric in Mainz, Germany. Leo X agreed to sell him the archbishopric. In an effort for Albert to raise the considerable sum, Leo X agreed that he could sell indulgences within his territory. The agreement, of course, contained a clause: of the funds secured, Albert would forward

2. Gonzalez, *Story of Christianity*, 2:19–20.

half to the pope's treasury. On his part, Pope Leo X wanted to finish St. Peter's Basilica, which Pope Julius II had begun. He had borrowed funds from the German Fugger Bank for the construction project, and needed to raise the needed funds. Through his financial receipts from the sale of the Mainz archbishopric and the indulgences, Leo X could pay back his bank loan. To get the best marketing for the indulgence sale, Pope Leo X arranged for an unscrupulous Dominican monk named Johan Tetzel to oversee the financial campaign. In return for his participation, the Dominican order would get a cut of the financial receipts. Tetzel even developed a catchy sales pitch: "As soon as the coin box rings another soul from purgatory springs!"[3] Albert, Leo X, and the Dominicans financially benefited from Tetzel's sale of these indulgences.

Luther and the Pope Collide

A Scholars' Discussion Turns into a Revolution

About the same time as this conflict was brewing, Martin Luther became a faculty member at the newly founded University of Wittenberg. Luther therefore challenged the Dominicans to a theological debate. He nailed his Ninety-Five Theses on the door of the Wittenberg church on the eve of All Saints Day in 1517. In these theses, Luther did not deny the right of the pope to grant indulgences. Rather, he felt that indulgences could not extend to purgatory. Luther even declared that if the pope could free people from purgatory, he should do it from the motive of love, not because of needing funds for a construction project. It is important to realize that in Luther's posting his Ninety-Five Theses, he was not rebelling against Rome and the pope. Rather, he was following a common practice among university scholars in initiating a debate. Ultimately, the debate did not take place, as elector Frederick the Wise previously had prohibited the Dominicans from entering Saxony. Some of Luther's students translated his Ninety-Five Theses into German and printed them along with the original Latin text. In turn, they were translated into many other languages. Due to the invention of the Guttenberg's printing press, the printed word propelled Luther's thinking onto the world stage. Further, with the German political structure fragmented into independent principalities, printing presses were located throughout the country. These scattered printing presses gave

---

3. Sunshine, *Reformation for Armchair Theologians*, 26.

greater freedom of expression than that found in nations with more centralized governments.

The criticism about the sale of indulgences led to a confrontation with the pope. Luther sent a copy of his theses and a respectful cover letter to Albert of Brandenburg. Albert angrily in turn sent the theses and cover letter to Rome, asking the pope to intervene. Likewise, the Holy Roman Emperor, Maximilian, was outraged at Luther's actions, and he wrote the pope asking him to silence the upstart monk. Shocked by the anger that he encountered, Luther wrote a clarification of the theological reasons behind the theses. The pope was not satisfied, and he told the Augustinian order quickly to deal with their disruptive monk. The Emperor Maximilian further summoned Luther to the next meeting of the Augustinian Order in Heidelberg. Only intending to have an intellectual debate with other theologians, Luther naively found himself over his head in conflicts. He was terrified and feared for his life. Yet his fellow friars supported him. Luther returned to Wittenberg, knowing that he was not alone in his search for truth.

Luther at the Diet of Augsburg

Realizing that the Augustinian Order was supporting Luther, the pope took a different tactic. The pope previously scheduled the diet, the regional governing body, to meet during October 1518 in Augsburg. The purpose of the meeting was to consider whether to undertake a crusade against the Turkish forces. The pope chose the Thomist scholar Cardinal Cajetan to attend the meeting in order to persuade the German princes to join the pope in the crusade. The pope gave Cardinal Cajetan additional instructions for the meeting. He was to either get Luther to recant his views or to seize him and to bring him as a prisoner to Rome. Frederick the Wise, the elector of Saxony, secured for Luther a safe conduct pass from Emperor Maximilian. A century earlier, a previous Holy Roman Emperor withdrew his safe conduct pass, and the Council of Constance burned John Huss at the stake. Even though Luther was fearful, he optimistically felt it was his duty to answer the charges against him. Therefore, he attended the meeting. The meeting did not go well for Luther. Cardinal Cajetan would not listen to Luther's views, and instead demanded that Luther recant his Ninety-Five Theses. When Luther realized that the pope gave the cardinal the authority to arrest him, he fled Augsburg at night and returned to Wittenberg.

The Reformation in Germany

Luther at the Leipzig Debate

Following his confrontation at Wittenberg, Luther reached a truce with the pope on the condition that he would abstain from inciting further controversy. The pope agreed to the truce with Luther because he wanted Frederick to be the next Holy Roman Emperor. Yet, due to the conflict stirred up by the religious differences, Duke George of Ducal Saxony called for a debate in Leipzig in 1519 to settle the theological differences. Presenting the traditional Catholic position was Johann Eck, a professor at Ingolstadt, and a member of the rival Dominican order. Representing Luther's theological assertions was Andreas Bodenstein von Karlstadt, a fellow professor at Wittenberg. In the debate, Eck hoped that he could manipulate Karlstadt into committing heresy, and thereby draw Luther into the conflict. The Augustinians were confident that the well-respected Andreas Karlstadt would clearly present the case. Eck turned out to be a far better debater than Karlstadt. By the second round, the Augustinians had replaced Karlstadt with Luther. Luther did well during the debate, although Eck forced him to acknowledge that his position was similar to that of Huss, whom the church had burned at the stake as a heretic. Hearing that some of Luther's positions were similar to that of Huss, Pope Leo X condemned Luther's writings and excommunicated him. In defiance of the pope, in 1520 Luther publicly burned the pope's order of excommunication. The pope then condemned Luther as an enemy of the entire Western church! Most scholars at the time would have agreed that Luther did not win the debate against Eck. Yet the debate sharpened Martin Luther's own theological thinking. As a result, Luther published six major theses attacking Catholic doctrine. Overall, Luther's teachings slowly were undercutting the church's authority.

Luther at the Diet of Worms

In 1519, the Holy Roman Emperor Maximilian died, and despite the pope's best efforts, Charles I of Spain became Charles V, the new Holy Roman Emperor. The geographic area of the Holy Roman Empire was composed of what today are the countries of Germany, Austria, the Czech Republic, Slovakia, and parts of Poland and Hungary. Unexpectedly, a few months before the diet was to meet, Pope Leo X died. Charles V then was able to get his mentor, Adrian of Utrecht, elected as Adrian VI, the last non-Italian pope until the twentieth century. Adrian VI would die a year and a half after his election and have little impact upon the church. In 1521, Charles V, the newly elected Holy Roman Emperor, summoned Luther to appear before the Diet of Worms. In order to persuade Luther to attend, Charles V gave Luther a safe conduct pass to attend the meeting. Luther felt great reservation concerning his attending the meeting, not confident that Emperor Charles V would keep his word. Nevertheless, despite the personal danger, he decided to travel there to present his case. At the meeting that April, again the diet did not give Luther the opportunity to make his argument. Rather, the diet only gave him the opportunity to recant his views or else possibly suffer the same fate as Huss. Luther asked to sleep on his decision overnight. Charles V granted his request. The next day, when asked a second time if he would recant, Luther replied to his questioner, ". . . I am bound by the Scriptures I have quoted, and my conscience is captive to the Word of God. . . . Here I stand, I cannot do otherwise. May God help me. Amen."[4] Fortunately for Luther, Charles V kept his word and allowed Luther to leave the city. Yet within a month after Luther had left for home, the diet declared Luther to be an outlaw, and ordered that the church burn his books. This action occurred late in the meeting, and many of the members of the diet already had left for home. Concerned for Luther's safe return, Elector Frederick sent armed men to intercept him on his journey homeward. They secretly took him to the safety of Wartburg Castle. In order to prevent a leak about his location from the royal court, Elector Frederick had previously told them that he did not want to know where they had taken Luther. Martin Luther remained at Wartburg Castle for ten months, translating the Bible into German. The castle, sitting on a hill far above the city of Eisenach, was a familiar sight from his early childhood. Because of his excommunication, the church removed Luther from his teaching post at Wittenberg. After his time of self-imposed exile, he began covertly wandering from town to town, wearing only the clothes of a peasant.

Luther Urges Moderation in Liturgical Changes

Luther would appear in public once again a year later to help resolve a dispute that he had initiated. In his earlier book *Address to the Christian Nobility*, Luther, infuriated by the shrines dedicated to the Virgin Mary, declared that his followers should destroy all such shrines. One of Luther's supporters, Andreas von Bodenstein of Karlstadt, went further, in declaring that

4. Ibid., 34–35.

true believers should destroy all religious art. By the end of January 1522, the Wittenberg citizens had wrecked their churches. In March, Luther returned to Wittenberg wearing only a monk's gown, and preached a series of sermons calling for restraint. Because of Luther's preaching, the citizens ejected a number of the religious fanatics from town.

Yet others persisted in their fanatical actions. Therefore, in 1523 Luther issued the following instructions regarding worship:

1. "There should be no worship without a sermon,
2. Daily services of the Word to be added to the weekly Mass.
3. The congregation must be present and participate in worship.
4. Hymnody should be written and sung by the people.
5. The people must notify the minister and be examined in their faith if they intend to take communion."[5]

Luther understood worship as God's gift to humanity, not a means to earn favor with God. Therefore, worship was not to incorporate any liturgical actions implying that the congregation was making a sacrifice unto God. At the same time, Luther was a pragmatist. In his 1532 German Mass, he thus retained many of the elements of the medieval Mass, such as images, liturgical vestments, altars, and candles. Luther knew that people need a sense of continuity in their daily lives, and too many changes can be overly traumatic for some.

Luther's major changes in the church's liturgy include the following:

1. "The elimination of the offertory.
2. An extensive paraphrase of the Lord's Prayer.
3. An exhortation for the right reception replacing the preface in the order for the Mass.
4. The elimination of the prayer of consecration in the service for Communion; only the words of institution were spoken as the elements were distributed."[6]

---

5. Rice and Huffstutler, *Reformed Worship*, 28.
6. Ibid., 28

The Peasant Revolt

In 1524, the year opened with unusual astrological events suggesting to astrologers a foreboding future. As a result, some 160 new tracts and almanacs soon were published predicting gloom and doom. In addition, a severe July hailstorm seemed to confirm predictions that the world was about to end. All of these factors contributed to the emotional climate that provided fertile ground for the Great Peasants' Revolt. The centers of the Peasants' Revolt were the same areas where Lutheran religious fervor was the strongest. In 1525, the peasants demanded twelve socioeconomic changes. Among their demands were the following:

> . . . relief from their economic plight—an end to serfdom, increased hunting and fishing rights, impartial law courts—as well as religious reforms, such as the right to select their own pastors, the right to collect their own tithes (the ten percent of their produce they owned to the church), and the right to select their own bishop. (Actually, it is not clear the peasants really wanted these religious reforms; they may have been added by the clerics who acted as the peasants' spokesmen.)[7]

At first, Luther tried to take a neutral approach, feeling sympathy with the desires of the peasants for a better life. Yet he also felt that rebellion against the established authorities was sinful. In time, the peasants' violence increased against the authorities, and disorder seemed to threaten Martin Luther's desire for an orderly world. He therefore responded in turning against the peasants' cause, writing a pamphlet titled, "Against the Murderous and Thieving Rabble of the Peasants." Eventually, the German princes stamped out the revolt with much bloodshed. Luther's opposition to the Peasants' Revolt diluted his support by the masses, as well as provided fodder for his opponents. Further, during these trying days, in 1525, his protector Elector Frederick died. To Luther's relief, Frederick was followed by his brother John "the Steadfast," a committed Lutheran who continued supporting Luther and his followers.

Luther's Marriage and Health Concerns

With Elector Frederick's support, Luther and his supporters closed the monasteries and convents around Wittenberg, and encouraged the monks

---

7. Sunshine, *Reformation for Armchair Theologians*, 57.

and nuns to get married. After two years, only one of those nuns had failed to either get married or return to live with their families. That one nun was Katherine von Bora (1499–1552). She was twenty-six years old at the time, an advanced age that society considered too old for marriage. Luther attempted to be a matchmaker for her but without any luck. Finally, the fifty-two-year-old Luther and twenty-six-year-old Katherine were married in June 1525 by Johannes Bugenhagen, his spiritual advisor and the minister of the city church. Katherine and Martin had a loving relationship, and Luther used to refer to her as "Katie, my rib." The stress of being a controversial figure in public life began to show in his declining health. In 1527, Luther developed cardiac symptoms and throbbing headaches. Wearing glasses for a number of years, by 1546 his sight in his left eye deteriorated significantly. Throughout the remainder of his life, Martin Luther suffered from gout caused by renal colic, the passing of several stones, constipation, a fissure, internal hemorrhoids, arthritis in his left hip, and high blood pressure. However, he attempted to carry on with his ministerial duties despite these painful afflictions. Overall, however, whenever Luther was feeling well, he possessed a warm and magnetic personality, a fine memory, a sense of humor, and exhibited a vivacious and confident demeanor.

Luther Prejudicial Attitude Concerning the Jews

History shows that many great men and women, though possessing great virtues and revealing brilliant insights into God's will for creation, likewise have great failings in their judgments. Such was the case of Martin Luther and his understanding of the role of the Jews in the world. In his early career, Martin Luther had argued that Jesus was a Jew, and that in time the Jews would convert to Christianity. However, by 1530, believing that God's Last Judgment was coming upon the world, he was frustrated that the Jews had not yet converted to Christianity. Therefore, in his 1543 tract "On the Jews and Their Lies," Luther urged Christians to burn down synagogues, confiscate Jewish literature, forbid their teachings, and take vengeance for their killing of Christ. Luther's writings served as the blueprint for the 1938 Nazi Kristallnacht ("Night of the Broken Glass").[8] Pastorally, we might understand his comments in the light of his significantly declining health and advanced age. Nevertheless, the later use of his tract for Nazi propaganda

---

8. MacCulloch, *Reformation*, 689–91.

is a reminder that prejudiced comments and articles often leads to unintended evil consequences.

The Great Reformer Dies

Luther, at sixty-three years old, during a bitterly cold winter, traveled to Eisleben some eighty miles away in an attempt to settle a disagreement between two brothers over their business. He took with him on his journey his three sons, so they might see the town where he was born and baptized. On the way, he fainted from shortness of breath, complaining of his left arm feeling stiff, and his chest having tightness. After resting, he continued on his journey. Arriving at Eisleben, he continued to feel ill. He had physicians summoned. Early on the morning of February 18, 1546, Martin Luther died of myocardial infarction. Four days following his death, his funeral and burial took place within the Castle Church. His close friend Philip Melanchthon delivered the eulogy, and the parish priest at Wittenberg delivered the sermon. His last years had been difficult for Luther due to his poor health, his conflicts with other reformers over the direction of the church, and his disappointment that he had not made a greater impact on transformation of the church. At the same time, these last few years he lived a happy home life with Katherine, the love of his life. She would survive him by six years. Even though Luther did make some changes in society, he was not a social reformer as John Calvin or John Knox. Yet, Luther laid the foundation for those who would follow him.

Philip Melanchthon

Melanchthon was born in 1497, in Bretten, in southwestern Germany, the nephew of the famous Catholic humanist Johannes Reuchlin. His father served as an arms maker for the elector. In accordance with German practice, he translated his German name into the more elegant-sounding Melanchthon. In 1509, he began his studies for a baccalaureate degree at Heidelberg. During his studies, he became an admirer of the works of the Swiss scholar and pastor Geiler von Kaysersberg. Because of his admiration, Melanchthon composed a poem in memory of his spiritual mentor. Transferring to Tubingen in 1512, he completed his master's degree two years later. In 1518, appointed at twenty-one years of age, Melanchthon served as the professor of Greek at Wittenberg University, where Martin

Luther likewise taught. They soon became close friends. As friends, Melanchthon and Luther were a study in contrasts. Melanchthon was retiring and timid, and yet of greater scholastic ability than was Luther. Melanchthon, however, was committed to furthering his friend's seminal ideas. In 1521, Melanchthon published *Loci Communes*, which would become his most important theological work. Melanchthon differed from Luther in his interest in the field of ethics. Whereas Luther felt that one's knowledge of the law could guide Christians in their ethical decision making, Melanchthon felt that churches needed to give clear directions as to ethical choices. Despite his great intellect, according to Luther, Melanchthon had a naïve trust in astrology. He once refused a call to travel to England due to the superstitious thought that he would die on a sea voyage.

Following Luther's death, Melanchthon came under attack from conservative Lutherans. In particular, Nikolaus von Amsdorf challenged Melanchthon's disagreement with Luther's affirmation of predestination. In his disagreement with Luther, Melanchthon felt that human "free will" had an important role in one's salvation. Andreas Osiander likewise challenged Melanchthon's teachings on justification, feeling that Melanchthon did not faithfully represent Luther's thinking on the subject. Further, strict Lutherans challenged Melanchthon on his understanding of the Lord's Supper. These strict Lutherans felt that they should treat reverently the bread and wine remaining after the celebration of the Lord's Supper. However, Melanchthon felt that, as they remained common bread and wine, no special treatment was necessary. Melanchthon was willing to compromise on the non-essentials of his theology for the sake of ecumenical cooperation. For example, he was willing to permit people to profess a Protestant understanding of the Lord's Supper while still being able to retain in worship the Roman rite. Stricter Lutherans rejected such compromises. Melanchthon grew weary of such divisive theological arguments, yearning only for the life of a professor of Greek and the classics. In the end, he died peacefully in his home in 1560. In 1577, the Formula of Concord resolved the struggle within Lutheranism.

Charles IV and the Schmalkaldic League

Even though the diet had approved an edict against Luther, no one was willing to enforce it. Then in 1526, the Diet of Spires formally withdrew the edict that the Diet at Worms had approved, instead opting for each prince to determine his own religious allegiance. The Holy Roman Emperor was very upset with the local option arrangement, and decided to intervene. In 1529, at the Second Diet of Spires, due to the threat of intervention by the Holy Roman Emperor, the diet reversed its previous action, and reaffirmed the edit of the Diet of Worms against Luther. The Lutheran princes protested their action, from which the princes received the name "Protestants." Sensing rebellion within the empire, Emperor Charles V returned in 1530 for the meeting of the Diet of Augsburg. At that meeting, Philip Melanchthon presented to the princes the Augsburg Confession, which summarized Lutheran doctrinal emphases. Although some of the Protestant princes disagreed on some points, in the end, they approved the document in a united political front against the Roman Catholic Holy Roman Emperor Charles V. The emperor was outraged, and the future of German Protestantism was uncertain. The princes therefore decided that only united could they withstand the overwhelming military forces of Charles V. They proposed the formation of a Schmalkaldic League as a defensive pact. Luther was reluctant to approve such a pact, given his understanding of Romans 13. However, in the end he consented to the formation of a defensive pact. In 1531, eight Lutheran princes and representatives of eleven imperial free cities formed the Schmalkaldic League. War soon broke out between Charles V and the Schmalkaldic League. However, due to the need for joint Roman Catholic and Protestant military actions in the defense of Vienna against Turkish forces, the war eventually ended in 1532 with the Peace of Nuremberg. Only when faced with a common enemy did they temporarily achieve a common unity.

However, peace did not last for long. In 1546, Charles V again was at war with the Schmalkaldic League. Although the league had a superior number of troops, their commanders had to consult with a Council of War on military actions. The dysfunctional leadership structure gave Charles V a great military advantage. In 1547, an army under the leadership of the brilliant commander, Fernando Alvarez de Toledo, the Duke of Alva, defeated the forces of the Schmalkaldic League and captured its leadership. In response, nearly all of the German cities submitted to the authority of Charles V, with the exception of Magdeburg and Bremen.

Failing to get the Council of Trent to resolve the conflict between German Lutherans and Catholics, in 1548 Charles V called a meeting of Protestant and Catholic representatives to draw up the Augsburg Interim. This document granted some concessions to Protestants. However, no one fully was satisfied with the results, and none of the recommended practices took effect. Approved later that same year, the Leipzig Interim had limited success in northern Germany.

Due to resentment over the Spanish enforcement of the Leipzig Interim, several Protestant princes reestablished the defunct Schmalkaldic League. The League, in an alliance with Henri II of France, was able to secure financial support. A second Schmalkaldic War soon broke out, with a combined force of Protestant and French troops in opposition to Charles V. In the face of such overwhelming military superiority, Charles V fled. The Diet of Augsburg met in 1555, and concluded the Peace of Augsburg. Its terms allowed each ruler being able to determine the faith of his own territory. As only Lutheran Protestants were included under its provisions, it did not address the freedom of worship for Calvinists, Anabaptists, or other religious groups. In time, the Peace of Augsburg ended the influence of the Holy Roman Emperor. Charles V abdicated in 1556 in favor of his brother the Spanish King Ferdinand. Charles V further granted Ferdinand territories in Austria. To his son Philip, Charles granted territories in the Low Countries, Spain, Italy, Africa, and the New World. Afterwards Charles V retired to Spain, and in 1558 he died.

The Heidelberg Catechism versus the Augsburg Confession

Meanwhile, Frederick III, "the Pious," had been reared a Catholic. However, he had converted to Lutheranism in 1546 and Calvinism in 1561, following his marriage to Princess Maria of Brandenburg-Kulmbach. A strong Lutheran, she influenced Frederick in his study of Lutheran doctrine. Philip Melanchthon became one of Frederick's trusted advisors. Once, in advising Frederick concerning how to resolve an ongoing conflict in his territory, Melanchthon told him, "In all things seek peace and moderation. This is done best by holding carefully to a fixed doctrinal position as regards the Lord's Supper and all other matters of faith."[9] Seeking to follow Melanchthon's advice, Frederick turned to two scholars at that university, Kaspar Olevianus and Zascharias Ursinus, to write a new catechism. He hoped that this new catechism would provide for conformity in teaching the essentials of the gospel. Frederick personally supervised the writing process, and at one point ordered the composers to rewrite some of the answers. Frederick felt that they too closely identified with controversial Zwinglian

---

9. "Introduction to the Heidelberg Catechism", *Book of Confessions*, 51–53.

language. In January 1563, the synod adopted the Heidelberg Catechism. It would undergo three revisions later that same year. The final and fourth edition included a book defining proper church order and liturgy for the Palatinate congregations.

Whereas Frederick had intended to bring peace to the church in supporting the Heidelberg Catechism, he ended up causing division and strife. Some leaders claimed that Frederick had deposed the Augsburg Confession's authority with the churches. The Roman Catholic Holy Roman Emperor Charles V, sensing a fracture in the Protestant coalition, summoned him to appear before the German diet in 1566 to answer to the charges. When Elector Frederick appeared at the diet, his son accompanied him, carrying symbolic copies of the Augsburg Confession and the Bible. Frederick confessed before the body, "What men know of Calvinism, I do not know. I can say with pure conscience that I have never read Calvin's writings. As to the . . . Augsburg Confession . . . that I signed with the other princes . . . in that faith I continue firmly on no other ground than that I find it established in the Holy Scriptures." Frederick further defended the Heidelberg Catechism, declaring, "My own catechism is drawn word from word from divine, not human sources, as the references from the margins will prove . . . If any person, regardless of age, station, or class, even the humblest, can teach me something better from the Holy Scriptures, I will give him hearty thanks and be readily obedience to divine truth . . . Here are the Scriptures . . . Would it please your Imperial Majesty to do this I would take it as a divine favor."[10] As his defense was impressive, no one responded to his request. The diet acquitted Frederick of all charges against him. Following Frederick's defense and the diet's action, the popularity of the Heidelberg Catechism increased among Reformed congregations.

---

10. Ibid., 53.

4

The Reformation in Switzerland

Huldrych Zwingli

The Early Years

CHIEF AMONG THE GERMAN-SPEAKING Swiss reformers was Huldrych (or Ulrich) Zwingli. Zwingli was born to Ulrich and Margaretha Zwingli in 1484, on a farm in the small eastern Swiss village of Wildhaus. His father was the village bailiff and a shepherd, and therefore Zwingli grew up under comfortable circumstances. While tending sheep with his father on the beautiful steep slopes of the Alps, Zwingli developed a love for his country that he would express through his deep sense of patriotism. An uncle, the dean of Wiesen, saw that Zwingli had the opportunity to receive the finest humanist education. Zwingli therefore studied for two years at the University of Vienna, followed by studies at the University of Basel at which, in 1506, he was awarded a master's degree. Following his academic theological studies, he was ordained as the parish priest of his boyhood church, the Glarus parish in Zurich. Zwingli was well suited for his congregation, and he took his priestly duties very seriously.

Zwingli's Pastoral Ministry

Over the years, foreign rulers had come to recognize the Swiss military as among the best in the world. They therefore sought after their service as mercenary troops. In 1513, as a reward for his affirmation of Swiss troops serving as mercenaries in support of the pope's military campaigns, the pope granted Zwingli financial aid. As their field chaplain, in 1512 and

1515, Zwingli accompanied the young men in his parish during several papal military campaigns. The French king likewise sought to employ Swiss mercenary troops for his own military ventures. Yet Zwingli spoke out against using Swiss troops in the service of other nations. In retaliation for Zwingli's outspokenness, French government supporters stirred up discontent within Zwingli's Glarus parish. Recognizing the extent of the discontent, he also assumed preaching duties at the historic shrine at Einsiedeln. In 1516, the Glarus parish asked for his removal as their pastor.

In 1518, Zwingli received word that the Great Cathedral in Zurich was seeking a pastor. The Great Cathedral, an ancient church, traces its origin going back to the time of Charlemagne in 1090. The bishop installed Zwingli as pastor on his birthday, January 1, in 1519. In a break with tradition, Zwingli resolved to preach through the entire New Testament, in contrast to using the lectionary. It took him six years to preach completely through the New Testament verse by verse.

In contrast to Luther, Zwingli had a greater comprehension of and appreciation for humanistic thought. In seeking to increase his understanding of the early Christian church, he corresponded with Erasmus and other humanist thinkers of that time. He likewise became familiar with Luther's writings. Zwingli especially appreciated Erasmus's emphasis that God wills for the church to be a positive instrument in improving society, as well as for the Holy Spirit to be active in the church's life. Further, Zwingli began to lead his congregation in serious Bible study. Zwingli purchased a copy of Erasmus's Latin New Testament translation. Yet Zwingli was not satisfied with reading someone else's translation of the biblical text. He therefore taught himself to read Greek, as well as purchased a copy of Erasmus's 1516 edition of the Greek New Testament. In 1519, after narrowly escaping death from the bubonic plague, Zwingli became convinced that the church should require only that which was required in the Scriptures. Not finding in the Scriptures any justification for the church's requirement of celibacy, in 1522 he secretly married Anna Reinhart, a widow and a former nun. In addition, Zwingli could not find in the Scriptures the church's requirement for fasting. Therefore, during a required season of fasting, he ate sausage at a gathering in the home of the town printer. When it became public, Zwingli responded by preaching a series of sermons against such prohibitions such as eating meat during Lent. His bishop, the bishop of Constance, was very upset with Zwingli's actions. He therefore he appointed a commission to correct the teachings of his renegade priest. The bishop's efforts to silence him only increased Zwingli's rebellious spirit.

The Reformation in Zurich

By 1523, Zwingli approached the Zurich city council with his concrete proposals for the church's reformation, which they approved. Worship, he felt, should focus on the reading and the hearing of God's Word through the sermon, not on the celebration of the Mass or homilies on the examples of the saints. Therefore, in 1524, in midsummer, workers and officials locked the doors of all the churches in Zurich. They spent two weeks transforming the sanctuaries toward the hearing and preaching of the Word, dismantling statues of the saints and discarding art works. Although Zwingli was a talented musician, he was concerned that the pipe organ might become an idol for the congregation. He therefore had them dismantled and removed from the sanctuaries. From that point forward, the congregation would sing the Psalms without the aid of musical instruments. In addition, the city council outlawed fasting, clerical celibacy, as well as the charging of fees for administering the sacrament of baptism and conducting funerals. The same year, as an example to other priests, he also publically married his wife. In 1525, the city leaders abolished the Catholic Mass. They replaced the Mass with a simpler Communion service. It emphasized that Christ spiritually was present with the congregation during the celebration of the Lord's Supper. Oddly, the service retained the Hail Mary and the commemoration of the dead. Worship ended with a prayer of confession and assurance of pardon that followed the sermon. In addition, the minister was to conduct the celebration of the Lord's Supper at a separate time other than the regularly scheduled Sunday worship service, as to give priority to preaching. In stressing the importance of education, in 1525 Zwingli opened an academy. The primary focus was to teach the students how to read and interpret the Scriptures in the original languages. Following Zwingli's death, Heinrich Bullinger became the director of the academy.

Although Luther and Zwingli separately reached their conclusions on the need for church reform, their thinking agreed on many points. One of those agreements was on infant baptism. In 1522, Luther wrote Melanchthon in giving his support to infant baptism, arguing that baptism was similar to the Israelite rite of circumcision. Zwingli seized upon Luther's theological insight. Infant baptism therefore became an identifying mark of the Reformed Church in Zurich.

Zwingli further introduced congregational voting to his congregation. He also developed regional assemblies at which elected lay and clergy commissioners would make decisions for common concerns within that particular region. His move was consistent with the other reformers who had a distrust of hierarchy.

Zwingli and Luther Differ Concerning the Lord's Supper

Although Zwingli and Luther found agreement on many points of doctrine, their differing understandings of the Lord's Supper would divide them. In 1529 Luther and Zwingli, in an effort to reconcile their differences, met in Marburg. At the meeting, they agreed on fourteen points of doctrine, but remained divided on the meaning of the Lord's Supper. Luther insisted that even though Christ remained in heaven, he still could be present in the elements of the Lord's Supper. To Zwingli, Christ only could be in one place—either in heaven at the right hand of God the Father, or on earth in the celebration of the sacrament. Zwingli therefore asserted that Christ spiritually was present in the midst of the celebrating congregation, but that Christ's body was not in the Communion elements. The purpose of the Communion elements was to lead the worshippers to focus on Christ's sacrifice, and to recall the historic events of our salvation. Luther responded to Zwingli's theological assertions by calling him "of the devil" and that he was nothing but a "wormy nut." Zwingli replied that Luther was treating him "like an ass." Their insults to one another ended all attempts at reconciliation. With the theological chasm between Luther and Zwingli regarding the meaning of the Lord's Supper, Reformed Protestantism had reached the point of defining itself apart from the Lutheran Protestant movement.

Zwingli's Contributions to Reformed Worship

Zwingli's significance for Reformed worship is as follows:

1. "He separated Communion from the normal Sunday worship.
2. His services set forth the centrality of remembrance for Communion; it is a memorial.

3. He abandoned the lectionary in favor of reading entire books of the Bible in sequence *(Lectionary continuo)*.

4. He rejected the physical world as revelatory or able to convey the spiritual, and thus he rejected visual symbolism (only the Word was salvific).

5. He was rigorously theological; even prayers were precise theological statements rather than simple devout petitions; that is, they were didactic rather than devotional."[1]

Zwingli Dies in Battle

In 1531, Zurich was at the height of its political power among the thirteen Swiss cantons. However, it misjudged the situation and overreached in seeking to force the Catholic cantons to accept evangelical preaching. War resulted, and on October 11, 1531, the Catholic forces defeated the Zurich army at Kappel. In the battle, the Catholic forces killed Zwingli. Because of its military defeat, Zurich had to dissolve its defensive pacts with the other Swiss cantons. Yet Zurich remained a Protestant city.

Heinrich Bullinger

Zwingli's son-in-law, Heinrich Bullinger, succeeded him as the pastor of the Reformed congregation in Zurich. Bullinger preached twice a week, wrote commentaries on most of the Old Testament books, and all of the New Testament books. The Book of Revelation had posed particular issues for Protestants and often resulted in extremist movements that focused solely on Christ's Second Coming. Bucer and Melanchthon sought to ignore the Book of Revelation, and Calvin rarely quoted from it. Archbishop Cranmer mostly omitted it from the 1549 lectionary. Yet Bullinger became the first Protestant leader to write a commentary on the book. He dedicated it to the English exiles in Zurich, who had fled there following Mary's 1553 ascension to the English throne. Bullinger's writings led to the Book of Revelation becoming a source of strength for persecuted Protestants.

In addition, he initiated the opening of a public school system and a theological seminary. Bullinger also wrote the Second Helvetic Confession,

---

1. Rice and Huffstutler, *Reformed Worship*, 30–31.

which was eventually adopted by the Reformed Swiss cantons as their confession of faith. Whereas Zwingli understood "covenant theology" based on Genesis 17, Bullinger had a more complex understanding of covenant theology that would find its' fulfillment in Christ's Second Coming. These Reformed leader's understandings of covenant theology would have social and political impacts for the Reformed church.

The Anabaptist Movement

For some leaders, however, Zwingli's changes were not severe enough. One such person was Conrad Grebel, who parted ways with Zwingli in 1523 over baptism. Grebel felt that since the Bible did not explicitly mention infant baptism, it could not be a sacrament. Adult baptism therefore was the only appropriate means of baptism. In January 1525, Grebel began rebaptizing adult church members in the fountain in the central square in Zurich. Heinrich Bullinger later would term Grebel's followers as "Anabaptist," meaning "rebaptizers". Approved in 1527, the Anabaptist Schleitheim Confession became the distinctive doctrinal standard of the Anabaptist movement. It advocated believers' baptism, banned from the church's fellowship those church members who had not repented of their sins, reserved the Lord's Supper only for believers, advocated separation from the evils within the world, elevated the clergy to serve as moral examples to their flocks, affirmed pacifism, and prohibited the taking of oaths. Soon the Anabaptists would shun the education of clergy, instead exhorting their ministers to rely only on the guidance of the Holy Spirit. Due to their stance on pacifism, many people felt the Anabaptists were not being supportive of the government. As a result, they began to suffer great persecution from local authorities. In 1525, the Catholic cantons of Switzerland began condemning to death Anabaptists, and the following year Protestant Zurich followed suit. Many of the Anabaptist martyrs were drowned, tortured to death, or drawn and quartered. Yet their movement grew. Under the leadership of Menno Simons, a former Catholic priest, the Mennonite movement began to assert itself. Disagreeing with the doctrines of infant baptism and transubstantiation, he also firmly held to the separation of church and state, and pacifism, principles established in the Schleitheim Confession. They established religious communities within the Rhine region, although some of his followers found a more accepting attitude in Switzerland. Jacob Hutter of Moravia led an even stricter group, known as the Hutterites. They affirmed believers' baptism, pacifism, and communal living. Eventually Roman Catholic authorities arrested him, and in 1536 burned him at the stake. Another Mennonite leader, Jacob Amman, in seeking to maintain purity from the evils of the world, led a Swiss Brethren congregation into Upper Alsace, Switzerland. Soon, however, hearing of the rich soil in America and the religious freedom in William Penn's new American colony of Pennsylvania, his group traveled there.

Martin Bucer

Born November 11, 1491, in Schlettstadt near Strasbourg, Martin Bucer's father worked as a cobbler. However, despite his humble birth, Bucer gained an excellent education at a Latin school in Schlettstadt. In 1506, at fifteen years old, he entered the Dominican cloister. In 1516, he transferred to the Dominican Blackfriars' cloister, where he read Erasmus's works. In 1518, Bucer attended a speech given by Martin Luther at the Disputation at Heidelberg that significantly helped shape Bucer's own theological understanding. By 1521, facing great opposition due to his changing theological beliefs, Bucer left the Heidelberg cloister in order to serve as a court chaplain for Franz von Sickingen. In an effort to lower the conflict level between Martin Luther and the pope, Bucer was involved in a plot to persuade Luther not to attend the Diet of Worms. Nevertheless, Luther remained unpersuaded, and did participate in the diet. Following the debate at the Diet of Worms in 1522, Bucer accepted a parish ministry in Landstuhl, a parish under the supervision of von Sickingen. While in Landstuhl, he married Elizabeth Silbereisen, a young nun.

Franz von Sickingen, his protector, met defeat in his military campaign against the elector of Trier. This event, in turn, made it necessary for Bucer to resign his pastorate at Landstuhl. Seeking a safe place for them to live, Bucer decided to move with his wife to Strasbourg, near her family members. Along the way, in Weissenburg, they met Heinrich Motherer, who persuaded them to remain there, and for him to serve the Saint John's congregation. However, their sanctuary in Weissenburg did not remain safe for long. Once again, the ongoing conflict between von Sickingen and the elector of Trier intervened, and the town council urged Bucer and Motherer to flee for their safety. In 1523 they quietly left Weissenburg. Martin and Elizabeth Bucer then moved to a new ministry in Strasbourg, where he served for the next twenty-five years. During his ministry at Strasbourg, he provided a middle way in the Reformation movement between the emphases of Zwingli at Zurich and Calvin at Geneva. In addition, when Calvin left Geneva, Bucer invited him to serve in Strasbourg. There Bucer served as a mentor to the younger theologian.

A deeply profound thinker, Bucer suffered from an inability to express his thoughts in a succinct manner. Luther even once referred to him as a "chatterbox"! Bucer emphasized God's benevolent love more than did any of the other reformers, and was able to see the good even in those persons who differed from him. A theological "bridge builder" throughout his life, he sought to bridge the expanding chasm between Protestantism and Catholicism. In addition, among his theological contributions, in his *Scripta Anglicana* Bucer he added to Calvin's two marks of the church—that "the Word of God being purely preached and heard, and the sacraments administered according to Christ's institution"—a third mark of church, that of "discipline." His emphasis on church discipline found support among those concerned regarding the behavior of church leaders. Bucer's third mark of discipline was included in the later Scots Confession and Belgic Confession of Faith.[2] Bucer further emphasized that the New Testament showed that there are four functions of ministry: pastors, doctors, elders, and deacons. John Calvin adopted Bucer's teachings on the first two of the marks of the church, as well as the four functions of ministry.

Bucer's Contribution to Reformed Worship

In 1524, Bucer developed an order of worship similar to that of Zwingli, but including a Declaration of Pardon and the reading of the Words of Institution during the celebration of the Lord's Supper. Then, in 1539, he developed his understanding of worship to include the following characteristics:

1. "He substituted the title 'Lord's Supper' for 'Mass'.
2. He called the altar the 'altar-table' or simply 'table'.
3. The priest became known as the 'parson' or 'minister'.
4. Vestments were abolished in favor of the academic gown.
5. The Gospel was read *Lectio continuo*, thus eliminating the lectionary.
6. The liturgical year was discontinued except for major festivals of Christ's life.

---

2. Calvin, *Institutes of the Christian Religion*, 1023 (footnote).

7. In place of the offertory, he used Romans 12:1ff—'self-sacrifice' to replace the idea of the sacrifice of the elements.

8. Weekly Communion was the rule, but by 1538, the practice of Morning Prayer and Sermon was developed for the parish churches that only celebrated Communion monthly. The cathedral continued to practice weekly Communion." [3] Perhaps due to his willingness to compromise, Martin Bucer failed to stand up to anti-Semitic attitudes. He once urged "Landgrave Philip of Hesse to allow Jews to reside in the electorate only under stringent conditions; for example, that Jews pledge not to harm Christians, refrain from religious disputes with Christians, be required to attend Christian sermons, discontinue using the Talmud, and engage in menial labor." [4]

In the spring of 1549, at the invitation of Archbishop Cranmer, Bucer fled Strasbourg for Edward VI's Protestant England. In 1550, he began lecturing at the University of Cambridge. Additionally, Bucer assisted Archbishop Cranmer in modifying the 1549 *Book of Common Prayer* and in the writing of the Articles of Religion. Feeling strongly that the state had an obligation to assist those in need, he had significant influence over the Elizabethan poor laws. Warmly received by the English people, he offered a gracious criticism toward the Roman Catholic Church, while also being critical of the extreme reformation measures of the Puritans. His motto was, "We believe in Christ, not the Church."[5]

Bucer died in 1551, after serving two years in England. Yet during those two years, Bucer had significant influence upon the English church and society. In 1556, the Catholic Queen Mary Tudor, in an effort to erase Bucer's influence, exhumed and burned his bones. However, her successor, Queen Elizabeth I, recovered his remains and reburied them in the Great Saint Mary's Church in Cambridge. James Atkinson wrote the following regarding Martin Bucer:

> Bucer was at home in Wittenberg, Zurich, Geneva, and knew intimately and personally the lives and works and thinking of the great Reformers. He was not only a conciliator between the Lutherans and the Swiss, but a reconciler of all those in southwest Germany who were neither Lutheran nor Swiss. He almost

---

3. Rice and Huffstutler, *Reformed Worship*, 31–32.
4. Ottati, *Theology for Liberal Protestants*, 107–8.
5. Atkinson, *Martin Bucer*, para. 13.

reconciled Roman Catholic Cologne with Protestantism. He was a theological bridge between the ferment of the Continent and the insularity of England.[6]

Following Bucer' death, Strasbourg adopted Calvinism. Eventually, the larger Calvinistic movement absorbed his brilliant theological thinking.

Guillaume Farel

Guillaume Farel, a former student of Erasmus, was born in 1489 in Gap, in the French province of Dauphine. Farel studied in Paris, where he would come under the influence of the humanist reformer Jacques LeFevre of Etaples. Due to his passionate Reformed preaching, Guillaume Farel eventually had to flee France for Basel. However, in 1524 he once again had to leave Basel due to his outspokenness. He traveled throughout Switzerland, without remaining in any one community for an extended period. During his travels, in September 1532 he preached to the Synod of the Waldenses in the Italian Cottian Alps. As a result, the Holy Spirit moved a larger number of the synod members to accept the Reformed faith. Later that year, Farel finally ended his travels with his arrival in Geneva. He began preaching the Reformed faith, but with limited success. Leaving town for what once again seemed greener pastures, Farel encouraged his friend Antoine Froment to travel to Geneva to proclaim the faith. Froment was able to secure a position as a schoolmaster. In January 1533, Froment preached a sermon that inflamed some of the citizens, and a riot ensued. By the following Easter, due to Froment and other Reformed preachers from Bern, citizens felt safe enough publically to celebrate the Lord's Supper. Due to political pressure from Protestant Bern, they also chose to break their military alliance with the Catholic city of Freiburg. That same December, feeling emboldened by the news of Froment's ministry, Farel returned to Geneva. In March 1534, Farel and others seized the Geneva Catholic Church, followed by the July 1535 seizure of the Catholic Church at La Madeleine and the August 1535 seizure of the Cathedral of St. Pierre. They abolished the celebration of the Mass and forced the monks and nuns to leave the surrounding monasteries. In May 1536, the Geneva general assembly officially adopted the Reformed faith. Due to the stress of his work, Farel's health declined, and he did not feel up to the task that lay before him. Therefore, on one evening, he

6. Ibid., para. 30.

persuaded a young Frenchman traveling through Geneva to remain there for the transformation of the church and society.

John Calvin

The Early Years

That young man was John Calvin, who would become the greatest systematic theologian of the Reformation. Calvin was born on the afternoon of Tuesday, July 10, 1509, in Noyon, France, twenty-five years after the births of Luther and Zwingli. Baptized at the parish church of St. Godebert, his parents named him after his godfather, John de Vatines, canon at the Noyon Cathedral. The fourth of five sons born to Gérard and Jeanne Le Franc Cauvin, John had four brothers and two sisters. Tragically, two of his brothers died while still young. Calvin was about five years old when his mother died. He remembered her as a beautiful and pious woman who had taken him to see the shrines of the Catholic saints. His father would remarry and they would have two daughters. In obedience to their father, his two remaining brothers received an education that would prepare them for the priesthood. Charles, his elder brother, became chaplain of the cathedral in 1518. Later deemed a heretic and excommunicated in 1531, he died in 1537. Calvin's younger brother Antoine, likewise was ordained a priest. With his younger sister Marie, he later embraced the Protestant faith and followed Calvin to Geneva in 1536. Antoine opened a bookstore in his adopted city. Through Calvin's influence, the people elected Antoine to public office. He married three times, fathering five children. His second marriage ended as he charged his wife with adultery. Certainly the scandal was an embarrassment for John Calvin. However, from all records Calvin silently suffered. Calvin's other sister married at Noyon and remained a Catholic.

Calvin's father was a notary, serving as the secretary to the bishop. As such, he was a part of the rising Swiss middle class. In an era when most people could not read or write, a notary would draft legal documents and witness contracts between persons. Through his father's business contacts, Calvin developed friendships with those in the upper strata of society. His father paid a fee for Calvin to receive an education along with the children of the powerful Hangest de Montmor household. When the bubonic plague struck Noyon, Calvin along with the younger Hangest children moved to Paris.

John Calvin's father, a strong-willed and opinionated man, desired for him to follow his elder brother Charles into the priesthood. In obedience to his father, on August 1523, at fourteen years of age, Calvin entered the University of Paris to study for the priesthood. That same year there was a severe outbreak of the bubonic plague. In 1528, he completed his undergraduate studies with an emphasis on Latin, philosophy, and dialectics. During his studies, he likewise became familiar with the writings of Wycliffe, Huss, and Luther. Meanwhile, in financing his education, a bishop who was a friend of his father named Calvin a priest in the diocese of Noyon. According to the terms of the appointment, Calvin never lived within the village or performed pastoral services. Instead, he paid an assistant to perform his duties. Calvin could use the remaining funds to pay for his own educational expenses.

By 1527, Calvin's father had a disagreement with the bishop over finances. He decided his son should cease his preparation for the priesthood and instead pursue becoming a lawyer. In obedience to his father, Calvin withdrew from his theological studies at the University of Orleans, and entered the University of Bourges. He pursued humanistic studies, particularly those stressing the reformation of society.

Calvin Theologically Moves toward Protestantism

At his father's death in 1531, Calvin felt free to determine his own life's vocational choices. He took up studies in Greek and Hebrew in the humanist College of France in Paris, which King Francis I had founded in 1530. In April 1532, the arrogant twenty-three-year-old Calvin, intent on correcting Erasmus's misinterpretations of Seneca, published at his own expense his first book, his commentary on Seneca's *De Clementia* (*On Clemency*). Calvin sent a copy of his book to Erasmus. He dedicated his book to his childhood friend Claude de Hangest, who at that time was the abbot of St. Eloy in Noyon. His writing reveals Calvin to be an orthodox yet progressive Roman Catholic theological scholar.

Between the spring of 1532 and 1534, Calvin felt his faith stirred by new insights. Possessing the potential of a brilliant career as a humanist, attorney, or churchman, his spiritual insights led him to risk it all in order to embrace the uncertain and persecuted Protestant movement. On November 1, 1533, his friend Nicholas Cop, the son of a famous physician, delivered his inaugural address as the newly elected rector of the University of Paris. In that address, Cop advocated religious reforms reflecting some of the writings of Erasmus and Luther. Calvin certainly had taken a hand in the writing of portions of Cop's address. The listeners were shocked and angered with Cop's radical ideas. With King Francis I supporting the persecution of the Lutherans, Cop and Calvin realized that their lives were in jeopardy. Hastily fleeing Paris, Calvin narrowly escaped arrest by descending from an upstairs window by tying bed sheets together. He made his way to safety disguised as a vinedresser, complete with a hoe as a prop. He visited Angouleme, where he met Jacques LeFèvre d'Etaples, a humanist who in 1512 had argued in his commentary on Romans for justification by grace through faith. He was living under the protection of Marguerite, the sister of Francis I. The following May 1534, Calvin traveled to Noyon to resign from his parish appointment. That same year he wrote his first theological work, titled *Psychopannychia*, published in 1542. *Psychopannychia* was an attack on the concept of "soul sleep," that is, the concept that following death our souls sleep until the Last Judgment. No longer feeling safe in France, in 1535 he settled in Protestant Basel, intending to live his life as a scholar. On the borders of Switzerland, France, and Germany, Basel was an exciting and eclectic city. Its printing presses had produced the first printed Greek New Testament. It likewise was the residence of the renowned scholar Erasmus. Calvin enjoyed the academic atmosphere of the city, reading widely from Protestant and Roman Catholic theologians, as well as studying the Bible in the Greek and Hebrew languages.

The Institutes of the Christian Religion

At twenty-seven years of age, in 1536, Calvin wrote a book to answer the false charges the Catholics were making against the French Protestant movement. He titled his book *Christianae Religionis Institutio*, which in English is titled *Institutes of the Christian Religion*. It was a short book of only 516 pages, six chapters in length, covering the subjects of the law, faith, prayer, the two recognized sacraments, the five false sacraments of the Roman Catholic Church, Christian freedom, as well as church and state. It would have been dangerous to possess a copy of his new book, therefore he printed it in a small format so that it could be concealed within one's coat pocket. Calvin sent a copy along with a very respectful introductory letter to Francis I. Seeking to promote a favorable response from the French king, he dedicated the book to Francis I. The first edition was a great success!

Written in Latin, the international language of scholarship, the book sold out in nine months. Over the next twenty-three years, Calvin would revise *Institutes of the Christian Religion*. It would become the clearest and most systematic theological writing of the Reformation movement. The final reorganization of the *Institutes* in the 1559 Latin edition followed the structure of the Apostles' Creed, consisting of 4 books, 80 chapters, and 1,521 pages. The French edition followed the next year.

In his theological masterpiece, Calvin was indebted to Luther for his concept of justification by faith, as well as his understanding of the sacraments as signs and seals of God grace. Like Luther, Calvin insisted on establishing the historical meaning of the biblical text. From Martin Bucer of Strasbourg, Calvin gained an understanding of God's glory displayed throughout creation. From Augustine, Calvin adopted the doctrine of election.

Calvin' Ministry in Geneva

In time, Calvin returned to France to settle some legal matters, as well as to convince his brother, Antoine, and his wife to join him in Basel or Strasbourg. However, the war interrupted Calvin's plans. Not able to travel the shorter route, the conflicting armies forced Calvin to travel by way of Geneva. In July 1536, John Calvin reached Geneva. He stopped at an inn for the night, fully intending to continue his journey the next morning.

Guillaume Farel, a French Geneva reformer, heard that Calvin was staying at the inn for the night. He visited with him. That fateful night, Farel persuaded Calvin to stay in Geneva and to be the spiritual leader of the Reformed church. The decision did not come easily, for Calvin strongly resisted the invitation. He kept insisting that he wanted to continue his travels in order that he might live the life of a scholar. Yet Farel's arguments prevailed, threatening Calvin with God's wrath if he refused to stay. Calvin took Guillaume Farel's words to heart and stayed. In a compromise with Calvin's wishes to have a teaching ministry, Calvin was not ordained as the "pastor" of the congregation. Instead, they employed him as a "doctor," responsible for giving daily lectures and preaching several times a week. On September 1, 1536, Calvin preached his first sermon as the new spiritual leader of St. Peter's Cathedral.

Calvin was an astute social reformer, having studied the theory of social transformation at the University of Bourges. He believed that the church has a duty to be a faithful steward of God's creation. He therefore persuaded the city council to close the city-sponsored houses of prostitution and to provide free public education for children. He refused to baptize children with the name Claude, the patron saint of Geneva. Unlike some other reformers, Calvin promoted the spirit of humanistic learning, including the teaching of math and science. Further, trained as a humanist, he appreciated biblical criticism, acknowledging biblical textual errors and incorrect chronology. He wanted his students to understand the Scriptures in their original context using the best scholarly tools available. While in Geneva, he also wrote the Geneva Confession, along with a catechism and a book of discipline.

Whereas Martin Luther later in his life joined with others to encourage the persecution of the Jews, John Calvin took a far more reconciling approach. In his commentary on Matthew 27:25, he reminded Christians that God established a covenant with the Jews through Abraham, and that God remained faithful to that covenant. Further, in his commentary on Romans 11:28–32, Calvin noted, "The counsel of God, by which he had once condescended to choose them for Himself as a peculiar nation, stands firm, and immutable."[7] John Calvin's comments reflected his high appreciation of the Hebrew Scriptures and of God's covenantal relationship with the Jews.

Given Calvin's temperament, eventually he conflicted with the local elite. They particularly disliked his opposition to sexually explicit dancing at weddings, and, his opposition to the naming of their children after one of the Catholic saints. Despite public opposition, on July 29, 1537, the city council followed Calvin's lead and prohibited these activities. However, in the first quarter of 1538 the political winds began shifting, resulting in the election of new council members. A conflict soon developed over whether the church could excommunicate unrepentant sinners. Calvin insisted that the church, not the city council, had the right and obligation to discipline church members. Soon afterwards, another issue—the issue of worship— came to the forefront. The city council favored the worship practices adopted by the Reformed city of Bern. Once again, in order to be consistent, he felt the decision to change the liturgy lay within the responsibility of the church's leadership. On Easter 1538, these snowballing conflicts came to a head. The city council ordered the Geneva ministers to use unleavened bread, as did the Bern church. Further defying the church's assertion that it possessed the sole right of church discipline, the city council refused to

---

7. Ottati, *Theology for Liberal Protestants*, 108.

restrict anyone from coming to the Lord's Table. Calvin and Farel refused to follow the city council's mandates due to the city council not having consulted with them prior to making these decisions. In order to prove their point, they decided not to serve anyone Communion that Easter. The following April, the city government fired Calvin and banished him from the city. As William Farel was in agreement with Calvin, he chose to leave for Bern. Calvin had been in Geneva slightly less than two years. At twenty-eight years old, he saw himself as a pastoral failure.

Calvin's Ministry in Strasbourg

Calvin, on Martin Bucer's invitation, traveled to the German-speaking city of Strasbourg to become the pastor of the Reformed church. Calvin hesitated to accept the position, unsure whether he wanted to assume another pastoral ministry. Bucer insisted that Calvin come to Strasbourg, warning him that he should not be like Jonah running away from the Lord's call. Calvin listened to Martin Bucer, as he had done with William Farel. In Strasbourg, he served a congregation of French refugees, as well as being a lecturer at the university. The congregation was small, with only four hundred members. Due to his low salary, he had to take in boarders. He preached four times a week, and provided pastoral care to those persons who were in need. Calvin also found time to enlarge his *Institutes of the Christian Religion*, as well as to write his commentary on Romans.

In time, the Strasbourg city leaders felt that Calvin should be married. However, Calvin enjoyed being a bachelor. Nevertheless, the city leaders insisted. Always the pragmatist, Calvin drew up a list of qualifications for his future wife. Some of those qualifications included that his new wife possess good housekeeper skills, have a pleasant personality, and display some concern for Calvin's increasingly poor health. After completing his list of qualifications, the interviews began. Calvin finally decided that the list was a waste of time. In August 1540, Calvin married Idelette de Bure, a widow with a teenage son and a younger daughter. Several years previously, Calvin had persuaded both Idelette and her now-deceased husband to switch from the Anabaptist movement to the Reformed church. Later, during her late husband's terminal illness, Calvin provided pastoral care to them. Following Idelette and John's marriage in 1542, she gave birth to a boy, Jacques, born premature, who died twenty-two days later. There followed several miscarriages. The pregnancies and birth experiences damaged Idelette de

Bure's body severely, and she died in 1549. Calvin never remarried. For the rest of his days, he mourned the death of his beloved wife.

Calvin Returns to Geneva

In Geneva, civic affairs deteriorated, as the city leaders faced pressure from Roman Catholicism. They wrote to Calvin in Strasbourg, asking him to help them to address the threatening accusations from Roman Catholic political leaders. He reluctantly agreed to do so. In 1539, he wrote his Reply to Sadolet, which answered assertions that Cardinal Sadolet made to the senate and people of Geneva. In appreciation for his intervention on their behalf, in the autumn of 1540 the Geneva city council asked Calvin to return as pastor. Calvin still was angry over their previous firing of him. He initially turned them down. They turned to William Farel in the hopes that he once again could convince Calvin to return to Geneva. Farel traveled from his church in Neuchatel to Strasbourg to meet face to face with Calvin. In the end, Calvin reluctantly consented to their request. In return, the congregation gave him a generous financial and housing package. One part of that financial package included the provision of two bottles of fine wine per day.

In his ministry at Strasbourg, Calvin changed. There he learned to control his temper and to negotiate differences with those who opposed his ideas. Before he accepted returning to Geneva, he wrote the city council telling them that he felt that the church order needed revising, and attached a copy of his proposed "Draft Ecclesiastical Ordinances." Yet he did not make their acceptance of these ordinances a condition for his return. Further, Calvin was willing to compromise with the city council concerning the issue of church discipline. The church consistory would exercise church discipline for certain moral offences. The exception was the excommunication of members, where the low council would make the decision after consulting with the consistory.

On September 13, 1541, Calvin returned to Geneva with his new bride. He picked up his ministerial duties where he had left off. The first item on his agenda when he returned was to teach a Bible study class. When he walked into the classroom, he remarked, "When we last met, we discussed such and such a verse; we now go on to the next (verse)."[8]

---

8. Sunshine, *Reformation for Armchair Theologians*, 133.

In Calvin's organizing the governance of the Geneva churches, he formed a consistory to have oversight of all of the Geneva churches. Composed of five pastors and twelve elders, the city council elected the elders on the consistory. Further, in adopting Bucer's model for the various forms of ministry, Calvin established four offices: pastors, doctors, elders, and deacons. The pastors were "to proclaim the Word of God, to instruct, admonish, exhort and censure, both in public and private, to administer the sacraments and to enjoin brotherly corrections along with the elders and colleagues." The doctors were to provide "instruction of the faithful in true doctrine, in order that the purity of the Gospel be not corrupted either by ignorance or by evil opinions . . ." The elders were "to have oversight of everyone, to admonish amicably those who are erring or to be living a disordered life, and when it is required, to enjoin fraternal corrections themselves and along with others." In describing the fourth order of office, that of Deacon, Calvin wrote, "There were always two kinds in the ancient Church, the one deputed to receive, dispense, and hold goods for the poor, but also possessions, rents and possessions; the other to tend and care for the sick and administer allowances to the poor. This custom we follow again now, for we have procurators and hospitallers."[9]

The Establishment of the Geneva Academy

Education was a high priority for Calvin. In particular, the education of ministers should provide at the least a lecturer in the Old Testament and in the New Testament. Prior to the establishment of the Geneva Academy in 1559, Calvin lectured in order to prepare ministers. Charles E. Raynal III has written, "The first building was completed in 1559 and the entire complex by 1562. The college consisted of classrooms, a great hall, and a courtyard planted with elms and linden trees. . . . It was built with some public funds, but the lion's share came through donations, large and small, given on the conviction that the destines of the church and of Geneva were linked to the school." In 1558, Theodore Beza was the first scholar to join Calvin at the academy, and in 1559 he became its headmaster. "He assisted Calvin in his lectures and taught Greek in the higher level courses, using Demosthenes and Aristotle in addition to the New Testament."[10] In desiring the

---

9. Calvin, *Calvin: Theological Treatises*, 58–66.

10. Charles L. Raynal III, "The Place of the Academy in Calvin's Polity," in George, ed., *John Calvin and the Church*, 127.

finest faculty for the academy, Calvin corresponded with several scholars in France asking them to serve. In addition, a number of dissatisfied faculty members from the academy in Lausanne came to teach at Geneva.

In addition, he lectured at the Geneva Academy in the preparation of future clergy. Beginning in 1546, he produced an average of more than one Bible commentary per year. While in Strasbourg, Calvin also learned the importance of pastoral care of his congregation. Therefore, when the bubonic plague struck in 1542, Calvin planned to join with the other five ministers in visiting the sick. However, the city council, aware of his declining health, ordered him not to visit persons that had contracted the plague.

Geneva became a city of refuge for those Protestants fleeing their homelands. However, over the years, this great influx of refugees threatened many of the natives of Geneva. They feared that these newcomers would change their established traditions. Their reaction threatened to undo all that Calvin had done. Calvin, however, was able to maintain his influence in Geneva. Then in 1553, the upcoming elections seemed to favor his opponents. Given his previous experiences in Geneva, Calvin was greatly concerned.

The Execution of Miguel Servetus

Yet, the arrival of the heretic Spanish physician Miguel Servetus saved Calvin and Farel's supporters from the jaws of serious political defeat. Living under the assumed name of Villeneuve, Servetus conducted a significant and innovative medical practice in Vienne, France. He likewise was fascinated with theology. As early as the 1530s, in his book, Servetus rejected the doctrine of the Trinity, comparing it to a "three-headed" mythological dog. Some scholars suggest that Servetus was seeking to find a mutually acceptable manner to dialogue with the Jewish and the Islamic communities regarding God's nature.

A brilliant but erratic thinker, Servetus began regular correspondence with Calvin. However, over time, their correspondence showed increasing differences over the doctrine of the Trinity. In 1553, Servetus wrote another book, again denying that Jesus was God, and arguing instead that he was a great human prophet. The Catholic Church arrested him, convicted him of heresy, and condemned him to burn to death at the stake. Escaping from his imprisonment, he fled to Geneva. Arriving in Geneva in August 1553, he attended the very church where Calvin was preaching. To his surprise, he was recognized and promptly arrested. Calvin recommended to the city council that they try him for heresy. The city council knew that during a trial Servetus might embarrass Calvin. Yet they knew that they could not ignore Servetus. Therefore, they administratively delayed the trial by writing various governments in Switzerland and other places, asking their advice on how to proceed with Servetus. All the governments agreed that the city council should try and, if convicted, put Servetus to death for heresy. During the trial, the city council served as the judges, with Calvin serving as the chief prosecutor. Calvin and the other clergy sought Servetus's execution by beheading. However, the city council refused. The following October 27, Miguel Servetus was burned at the stake in Geneva. Since then, Servetus's execution has placed a stain on Calvin's ministry. Yet, if the Calvinists had not executed Servetus, the Catholic Church certainly would have done so. In the end, Servetus's execution removed from the Reformed church any public opposition to the doctrine of the Trinity.

Calvin's Understanding of the Lord's Supper and Preaching

Due to his careful reading of the Eastern church fathers, Calvin gained a unique perspective on the meaning of the Lord's Supper. Luther insisted that Christ spiritually was present in the bread and the wine, even though the elements themselves did not change. Zwingli, at the other extreme, insisted that Christ spiritually was present in the faith of the worshipping congregation. Calvin agreed with Zwingli that Christ remained in heaven at the right hand of God the Father, and therefore could not be in the elements of the Lord's Supper. Yet Calvin went beyond Zwingli in his understanding of Christ's presence. Calvin said that since Christ could not come to earth in the sacrament, that Christ spiritually raises us into the heavenly realm, where we spiritually celebrate the Lord's Supper with Christ and the saints. Calvin thus understood the Lord's Supper as a foretaste of the heavenly banquet.

In the 1559 edition of his *Institutes of the Christian Religion*, Calvin wrote the following instructions concerning the administration of the Lord's Supper:

> But as for the outward ceremony of the action—whether or not the believers take it in their hands, or divide it among themselves, or severally eat what has been given to each; whether they hand the cup back to the deacon or give it to the next person; whether the bread is leavened or unleavened; the wine red or white—it makes

no difference. These things are indifferent, and left at the church's discretion.... Now to get rid of this great pile of ceremonies, the Supper could have been administered most becomingly if it were set before the church very often, and at least once per week. First, then, it should begin with public prayers. After this a sermon should be given. Then, when bread and wine have been placed on the Table, the minister should repeat the words of institution of the Supper. Next, he should recite the promises which were left to us in it; at the same time, he should excommunicate all who are debarred from it by the Lord's prohibition. Afterward, he should pray that the Lord, with the kindness wherewith he has bestowed this sacred food upon us, also teach and form us to receive it with faith and thankfulness of heart, and inasmuch as we are not so of ourselves, by his mercy make us worthy of such a feast. But here either the psalms should be sung, or something be read, and in becoming order, the believers should partake of the most holy banquet, the ministers breaking the bread and giving the cup. When the Supper is finished, there should be an exhortation to sincere faith and confession of faith, to love and behavior worthy of Christians. At the last, thanks should be given and praises sung to God. When these things are ended, the church should be dismissed in peace.[11]

Moreover, Calvin believed that the act of preaching was the Word of God. Therefore, he preached eight or nine times every two weeks, including twice on Sunday as well as some weekday mornings. On Sunday mornings, he preached on the New Testament, in the afternoon he preached on the Psalms, and on weekdays from the Old Testament. On some Friday evenings, he also preached for the ministers that gathered for worship. His sermons lasted about thirty minutes. He preached without notes, with Scripture readings directly translated from the Greek and Hebrew. John H. Leith writes:

> Calvin understood preaching to be a sacrament of the saving presence of God.... The power of preaching as the Word of God does not reside in the sound of the words themselves or even in their meaning. The power of preaching is the act of the Holy Spirit that makes the words, their sound and their meaning, the occasion of the voice of God. "If the same sermon is preached, say to a hundred people, twenty receive it with ready obedience of faith, while the rest hold it valueless, or laugh, or hiss, or loathe it." Yet the

---

11. Calvin, *Institutes of the Christian Religion*, 1421–22.

ultimate difference in the response does not reside in the sermon, but in the electing grace of God.[12]

Calvin and Illness

During the last twenty-three years of his short life, Calvin struggled with a number of ailments and illnesses. His own frail health contributed to his thinking about the human afflictions of bodily weakness, fatigue, aging, illness, and death. For example, in a sermon on Job delivered when he was forty-five years old, he preached the following: "... that I may see my body decaying. If any strength remains, it declines from day to day, and I contemplate death without having to seek it ten leagues away."[13] Despite his physical decline, Calvin remained productive for another ten years. He saw his illness as a wakeup call to get his priorities in order to be ready when death arrived. Among his many ailments and illnesses, he suffered from chronic gout, kidney stones, urinary retention, severe hemorrhoids, nephritis, chronic pulmonary tuberculosis, intestinal parasites, spastic bowel syndrome or an irritable colon, and severe migraine headaches. In addition, he suffered from several bouts of influenza, and malaria. The last ten years of his life, he ate one meal a day. Calvin remained a workaholic, working until late at night and rising early to continue his writings. As early as 1563, gout and arthritis periodically had made it impossible for him to walk. His fellow ministers implored him to take more rest. Yet Beza his close friend reports that Calvin responded, "What! Would you have the Lord find me idle?"[14] While the effects of hemoptysis, a symptom of his tuberculosis, confined Calvin to bed, he dictated his final edition of the *Institutes of the Christian Religion* in Latin. He followed his Latin edition with one in French. He further revised his commentary on Isaiah, and reviewed his lectures on the Minor Prophets. A Spirit-driven man, John Calvin worked until only eight days prior to his death. Toward the end of his ministry, men had to carry him in a chair into the elevated pulpit to preach. On May 2, Calvin wrote his friend William Farel a farewell note. Farel, although seventy-five years old and in frail health, nevertheless traveled to visit with

12. John H. Leith, "Calvin's Doctrine of the Proclamation of the Word," in George, ed., *John Calvin and the Church*, 211.

13. Charles L. Cooke, "Calvin's Illnesses and Their Relation to Christian Vocation," in George, ed., *John Calvin and the Church*, 59.

14. Godfrey, *John Calvin*, 195.

Calvin for one last time. Calvin died peaceably at fifty-seven years of age, on Saturday, May 27, 1564, at 8 o'clock in the evening, the same year that William Shakespeare was born. The cause of death most likely was septicemia or pulmonary tuberculosis. His friend Theodore Beza conducted his funeral. They buried John Calvin in an unmarked grave in Genevan Plein Palais' cemetery. Calvin had rejected the idea of the superstitious veneration of the dead, and wanted no pilgrimages to his grave.

John Calvin in his ministry wrote commentaries on all the books in the Bible, with the exception of Second and Third John and Revelation. He wrote and re-edited numerous times the *Institutes of the Christian Religion*. In addition, he wrote the Geneva Confession and Geneva Catechism, and a Book of Discipline. Simply the massive volume of his writings testifies to his passion for teaching and preaching the gospel. His passion for the gospel remains an inspiration today for all of us.

Theodore Beza

Theodore Beza was born June 24, 1519, in Vezelay, in the northern-central French Burgundy region. His father was Pierre de Beza, a bailiff and the descendant of a prominent family. His mother was Marie Bourdelot, whom people recognized for her intelligence and commitment to charity. His mother died when he was three years old. As his father was unable to care for the boy alone, his uncle, Nicolas de Beza, a member of the "Parlement in Paris," took the boy to Paris to live with him. He sought to provide Theodore with the best education possible. At his uncle's urging, Beza studied humanities and law at the University of Orleans. Receiving his law degree in August 1539, he returned to Paris to practice law. In 1548, Beza suffered a serious illness, during which time he began to focus his energy on life's spiritual questions. Breaking off his law practice, Beza and his fiancée, Claudine Denosse, traveled to Geneva so that he might study under Calvin. Impressed by his gifts of scholarship and teaching, in 1549, Pierre Viret, a Protestant reformer, saw to it that Beza became the professor of Greek at the Lausanne academy. In 1559, Beza became the headmaster of the Geneva Academy. On Calvin's death, Beza additionally became the leader of Geneva's "Company of Pastors."

A renowned scholar, he edited an annotated text of the Greek New Testament, worked with Calvin in producing a French translation of the New Testament, wrote biographies of the reformers, and gave to Cambridge

University the *Codex Bezae*, one of the most important New Testament manuscripts. Committed to seeing the Reformed faith flourish in France, Beza traveled frequently there on behalf of the Reformation movement. He dedicated a French book of worship to Queen Elizabeth I, in hopes of encouraging her support of the Reformation cause in France.

Despite Beza's best efforts following Calvin's death, harassment by the Catholic duke of Savoy led to a decline in the Genevan population. The Geneva Academy began to lose some of the best students and faculty to Heidelberg University. Beza, having a very different temperament from Calvin, sought to be a reconciler between Protestant and Catholic theologians. In 1561, he participated alongside with Catholic and Protestant theologians in a theological dialogue in Poissy, France. Their decisions led to the 1561 edict by Catherine de Medici permitting Huguenots to assemble for worship, with the exception of within walled towns.

Beza's last years were difficult for him due to his partial loss of hearing, alongside increasing dementia. In 1588 his wife Claudine died. He married a second time, to Geneviève of Piano, the widow of a refugee from Genoa. Sadly, his increasingly poor health forced him to give up the duties for which he committed his life. In 1586 he ceased preaching daily, and by 1600 he preached only on Sundays. In 1598 he retired from the Academy and sold his library. On Sunday, October 13, 1605, he died. He desired burial in the public cemetery near the grave of his wife, yet the threat of desecration of his grave made necessary his burial in the cloister of St. Peter's Cathedral in Geneva.

The Passing of the Torch

The end of the decade of 1560s marked a watershed moment in the Reformation movement. Most of the imaginative original Reformation leaders were dead. It had been a generation since Zwingli's body lay dying on a battlefield near Koppel. In 1546, Luther, interned in the Castle Church, no longer was able to register his indignation at the later Lutheran schisms. Bucer died in 1551 at his teaching post in Cambridge. Melanchthon remained in Wittenberg until his death in 1560, scorned by those who claimed to be the purer guardians of Luther's legacy. His family buried him in the Castle Church near his mentor Martin Luther. By 1564, pulmonary tuberculosis or septicemia claimed Calvin. At his own wishes, his burial was in an unmarked grave. Bullinger led the Zurich Reformed church until 1575.

The Reformation in Switzerland

With Beza's death in 1605, the original reformers passed the torch of the Reformation onto a new generation of leaders. Some of their emphases in theology and polity would differ from that of the original reformers; nevertheless, they would remain true to the original vision. For example, Calvin's definition of the church in his *Institutes of the Christian Religion* was as follows: "Whenever we see the Word of God purely preached and heard, and the sacraments administered according to Christ's institution, there, it is not to be doubted, a church of God exists."[15] Although Calvin felt discipline was important for the church, he did not include it one of the marks by which to recognize the church. Calvin's restraint was due to his recognition that no pure church exists on earth. In accord, he wrote in the *Institutes*:

> Indeed, because they think no church exists where there are not perfect purity and integrity of life, they depart out of hatred of wickedness from the lawful church, while they fancy themselves turning aside from the faction of the wicked.
>
> They claim that the church of Christ is holy [Eph 5:26]. But in order that they may know that the church is at the same time mingled of good men and bad, let hear the parable from Christ's lips that compares the church to a net in which all kinds of fish are gathered and are not sorted out until laid out on the shore [Matthew 13:47–58] . . . [Matt. 13: 24–30] . . . [Matt. 3:12] . . . But if the Lord declares that the church is to labor under this evil—to be weighed down with a mixture of the wicked—until the Day of Judgment, they are vainly seeking a church besmirched with no blemish.[16]

Bucer, however, concerned over the ethical behavior of church leaders, in his 1577 *Scripta Anglicana* included discipline as one of the marks of the church. In turn, the later Scots Confession and Belgic Confession likewise included discipline as a third mark of the church.[17]

---

15. Calvin, *Institutes of the Christian Religion*, 1023.
16. Ibid., 1027–28.
17. Ibid., 1023 (footnote).

Portraits of Reformers

Desiderius Erasmus

Martin Luther

Portraits of Reformers

Huldrych Zwingli

Martin Bucer

Philip Melanchthon

John Calvin

Portraits of Reformers

John Knox

Theodore Beza

5

The Reformation in England, Scotland, Ireland, and Wales

The Reformation in England

Henry VIII

In Search of a Male Heir

The father of Henry VIII, Henry VII, in seeking a political alliance with Spain, arranged the marriage of his eldest son and heir to the throne, Arthur, to Catherine of Aragon, the fifteen-year-old daughter of Ferdinand and Isabella of Spain. However, six months later, in 1503, Arthur died. The Spanish king then proposed that their daughter marry Henry VIII, the younger brother, who now would assume the English throne. In order to overcome the obstacle of the ecclesiastical prohibition against marrying a brother's widow, a papal dispensation was required. With the papal dispensation secured, in 1509, Henry married Catherine of Aragon, and the political alliance between England and Spain was sealed. They had six children, of which only one, Mary, survived. However, the lingering question remained as to whether the pope had the right to grant the dispensation for them to marry.

As time went by, Catherine did not deliver a surviving male heir. Therefore, by 1527, Henry began seeking a means to dissolve his marriage to Catherine. Henry's concern was that without a male heir at his death, a civil war would break out in his country. Henry, a philanderer, likewise, fell in love with Anne Boleyn, a lady of the royal court. Despite Henry's request for an annulment of his marriage, Pope Clement VII did not want to anger

Charles V, who was Catherine's uncle and the Holy Roman Emperor. The pope therefore refused to dissolve the marriage. In January 1533, Henry married Anne Boleyn. In keeping everything legal, Thomas Cranmer, the newly appointed archbishop of Canterbury, issued a judgment that declared Henry's previous marriage to Catherine invalid. Cranmer's action in declaring the marriage invalid eventually would cost him his life by the hand of Mary Tudor, the daughter of Catherine of Aragon. In September of that year, Anne Boleyn bore a daughter, Elizabeth, who later would rule as England's queen. In 1536, Catherine of Aragón died of cancer.

Henry VIII Named the "Only Supreme Head" of the Church of England

In response to Thomas Cranmer's dissolution of Henry's marriage to Catherine of Aragon, Pope Clement VII in July 1533 excommunicated Henry. Henry answered the excommunication by refusing to send any future financial payments to Rome. Further, Henry declared that he alone had the authority to nominate all bishops. In November 1534, Parliament approved the Act of Supremacy, which declared that Henry VIII and all his future successors were the only "Supreme Heads" of the Church of England. In essence, the king had assumed the power of the pope. Sir Thomas More, a friend of Henry VIII, refused to recognize Henry as the Supreme Head. The king thereupon imprisoned Sir Thomas More in the Tower of London, and, in May 1535 the king executed him. In 1935, four hundred years after his execution, the Roman Catholic Church added Thomas More to its list of saints. Henry likewise executed a number of monks who refused to recognize his supremacy.

Henry's Wives Lose Their Heads for Want of a Son

Meanwhile, Anne Boleyn likewise failed to give birth to a male heir. In order to end their marriage, Henry charged her with adultery, and in May 1536 beheaded her. Her execution took place two days before Archbishop Cranmer could even declare their marriage invalid. Eleven days later, Henry married Jane Seymour, who later gave birth to a son, Edward VI. Tragically, because of the trauma of the birth, Jane Seymour died eleven days later.

Being politically astute, Henry knew that he needed political support from the German Protestants. In January 1540, Henry therefore married

Anne of Cleves, the sister of the Protestant Saxon elector. Later however, when he did not need Protestant support, Cranmer annulled their marriage. Unlike her predecessors, Anne wisely gave consent to the annulment. In turn, Henry gave Anne a generous financial settlement. Shortly thereafter, he married Catherine Howard, the niece of the duke of Norfolk. Yet, by February 1542, he questioned her ethical behavior, and beheaded her. In July 1543, he married Catherine Parr, who survived him. On January 28, 1547, the philandering Henry VIII finally died.

Edward VI, the Protestant Child King

The Early Years

Henry VIII had waited for twenty-eight years for the birth of a son. From the date of his son's birth on October 12, 1537, the king took every means to ensure that his son survived the perils of childhood. Henry's servants washed the walls and the floor of Edward's apartment three times a day, his food was fit for a prince, and a multitude of servants sought to meet his every need. Yet, despite the king's yearning for a son, Henry visited him infrequently. Further, Henry instructed the staff to send reports of Edward's welfare to Cromwell, the king's secretary. In addition, his two stepmothers, Anne of Cleaves and Catherine Howard, did not spend time with him. Only after the king married Katherine Parr in 1543 did Edward feel the affection of a mother.

Edward VI became heir to the throne at nine years old. The royal council thereupon established "regency." The royal council further appointed Edward Seymour, the eldest's uncle of Edward VI, to serve as the "protector." Fitting his new appointment, Seymour soon acquired the title of the Duke of Somerset. Edward contracted syphilis at birth and was a sickly child. Despite the lingering effects of his illness, he possessed a high intellect, with journal writing and fluency in Latin and Greek languages.

The Acts of Uniformity and the Books of Common Prayer

Edward Seymour had Protestant sympathies, and Edward VI became even more ferociously committed to the Protestant cause. He made significant Protestant reforms, including the giving of the cup to the laity, confiscating church properties, removing images from the churches, enabling priests to marry, and eliminating religious fraternities and guilds.

On January 21, 1549, Parliament approved the Act of Uniformity, requiring the use of the English *Book of Common Prayer*. An English revision of the older services written in Latin, the 1549 book was more accessible to worshippers. Revisions meant that the church calendar was simplified, the prescribed readings for each service revised from an eight-hour schedule to the simpler Morning and Evening Prayer; and whenever Holy Communion was celebrated, the minister was to preach a homily. Due to superstition, Parliament in the Act of Uniformity eliminated the use of holy water, ashes, and palms. Moreover, it prescribed readings from the Old and New Testaments at both services, and each month the reading of all 150 of the Psalms. Lastly, in seeking a moderating tone, Parliament prescribed that whenever the minister distributed the bread and wine to the communicants, his words of distribution would reflect the Catholic or Lutheran tradition.

The new *Book of Common Prayer* was not popular with the people. On June 10, the day after its introduction, in the conservative western counties riots erupted. In those cities with greater Protestant populations, particularly London, in 1551 and 1552 people likewise rioted due to the statues and ornaments remaining in the churches. Responding to the disorder, Parliament in its 1552 Act of Uniformity, revised the 1549 *Book of Common Prayer*. This revised 1552 version more reflected the Zwinglian tradition. For example, in the 1549 *Book of Common Prayer*, in giving the bread to the congregation, the minister would say, "The body of our Lord Jesus Christ which was given for thee, preserve thy body and soul unto everlasting life." In contrast, the 1552 version reads, "Take and eat this in remembrance that Christ died for thee, and feed on him with thy heart by faith with thanksgiving."[1] To define further the Reformed Communion service apart from a Mass, prior to the service the priest placed the bread and the wine on the table. Furthermore, the congregation placed the financial offerings for the poor into the "poorman's box," instead of placement on the Communion table. In addition, in the 1552 *Book of Common Prayer*, the church replaced the altar with a Communion table and substituted the wafers used in communion with ordinary bread. Whenever the people gathered for the celebration of the Lord's Supper, they sat at long tables, set up in the shape of a U or a T in the chancel or nave. Additionally, Parliament prescribed that the minister wear only a surplice, and the bishop a rochet, a long white

---

1. Gonzalez, *Story of Christianity*, 2:76.

vestment with gathered sleeves. It forbade the wearing of albs, chasubles, and copes. In 1553, the Church of England sanctuaries, with Scripture verses painted on white plastered walls, simple wooden Communion tables placed among the worshippers, and prominent pulpits as the central focus of worship, expressed the Church's theology.

Archbishop Cranmer appointed six chaplains to assist him in his work. One of those chaplains was John Knox, the Scottish reformer whose influence was in the inclusion of the "Black Rubric" in the 1552 *Book of Common Prayer*. It stated that "although kneeling was required for the sake of reverence and humility, kneeling to receive the elements implied no adoration of the elements nor transubstantiation."[2]

Further, an interesting change took place in the vows for the marriage service. The medieval marriage service included the woman promising to be "bonny and buxom in bed, and at the board." In contrast, the 1549 and 1542 revisions of the *Book of Common Prayer* required both partners to promise to "love, cherish, and obey," as well as "for better for worst, for richer for poorer, in sickness and in health."[3] Lastly, in 1553, the evangelical Archbishop Cranmer, along with his six court chaplains, prepared the Forty-Two Articles, a summary creedal statement.

Political Intrigue and the Death of Edward VI

Due to the political intrigue within the royal council, a rival of Edward Seymour, John Dudley, the duke of Northumberland, spearheaded the conviction of Edward Seymour, the "protector," on the trumped-up charge of treason, and execution of him in January 1552. John Dudley, although not assuming the position of the protector, thereafter became the most powerful man in Protestant England.

Reigning only six years, Edward VI died from tuberculosis in 1553, at fifteen years of age. A month following his death, he was embalmed and laid in a sealed lead coffin, and buried in Westminster. As his procession passed through London, many of the observers wept and lamented his death. One later wrote of the event that, "at his burying was the greatest moan made for him of his death as ever was heard or seen."[4] Archbishop Cranmer conducted his funeral service using the 1552 *Book of Common Prayer*. Although

---

2. Rice and Huffstutler, *Reformed Worship*, 39–40.
3. Skidmore, *Edward VI*, 8–9.
4. Ibid., 282–83.

Edward's reign was short in time, his contributions to the Protestant movement in England were significant. Edward VI commitment to the publication of the 1549 and 1552 editions of the *Book of Common Prayer* established a Protestant liturgical worship model that served as a bridge to the newer liturgical worship materials produced during the reign of Elizabeth I. As a testimony to his contributions, Elizabeth I declared that a portrait of Edward VI be printed on the frontispiece of the 1595 Bishop's Bible.

Catholic Mary Tudor: The Rightful Heir to the Royal Throne

Lady Jane Gray Lays Claims the Royal Throne

Mary Tudor (Bloody Mary), the daughter of Catherine of Aragon, was the rightful heir to the English throne. However, some of the Protestant nobles feared that Mary, a Catholic, would return the English Church to the Roman Catholic fold. Therefore, in a self-serving plot hatched by John Dudley, the duke of Northumberland, some of the Protestant nobles attempted to place the fifteen-year-old Lady Jane Grey on the throne. They claimed that since her mother was Henry VIII's niece, she was therefore the rightful heir. Dudley, in preparation for this occasion, persuaded the ill and dying King Edward VI to name Lady Jane Grey, his daughter-in-law, as Edward's successor. Her supporters proclaimed her queen in July 1553. However, the most prominent reformers refused to support such a blatant attempt to circumvent the divine right of kings. Thereupon, Mary Tudor, Edward's half-sister, the daughter of Henry VIII and Catherine of Aragon, and the rightful heir, assumed the English throne. With popular support of the Tudor dynasty, Mary's army easily defeated her opponent. Grey's reign lasted nine days. Mary Tudor's forces captured Lady Jane Grey and Mary sent her to the Tower of London. Attempting to show mercy to her captive, Mary simply demanded that Lady Jane Grey receive Mass; however, Lady Jane Grey refused. Mary's archbishop, Feckenham, further attempted to convince her to accept Catholicism. In February 1554, failing in their efforts to force her to betray her Reformed convictions, they executed her. However, prior to Mary's execution, they executed her husband, Guilford Dudley.

Mary Tudor Rightfully Recognized as Queen

On the previous August 1553, Mary made her entrance into London, accompanied by a thousand retainers, her half-sister Elizabeth, and 180 ladies-in-waiting. "Rich cloths and tapestries hung from buildings and between them, images of the Virgin Mary and other effigies of saints, now proudly restored from their hiding places, peered out from windows. On every crossroad, the banners proclaimed the same message, '*Vox populi, vox Dei*'—'the voice of the people (is) the voice of God."[5] Despite the celebration over her arrival, Mary remembered the public lament over the death of her half-brother Edward. She knew that Protestant plotters would seek to overthrow her reign. To secure the English throne against these potential political opponents, Charles V advised Mary Tudor to marry his son, and her cousin, Philip II of Spain, a member of the powerful Catholic House of Hapsburg. Yet, Philip felt no romantic interest in Mary, who was eleven years his senior. Nevertheless, politics trumped romance and they married. Yet, following their wedding in July 1554, Philip returned home to Spain. Only once did he visited Mary, in 1557 on a political mission. Despite her political intentions, her marriage to Philip II was very unpopular with her subjects.

Mary Tudor Restores Catholicism and Takes Revenge

Charles V, the Holy Roman Emperor, aware of the opposition that she faced, counseled Mary Tudor to move slowly in making religious changes. Disregarding his counsel, she quickly moved to return the Church of England to those forms of worship that Henry VIII approved. She restored the saints' feast days, and ordered married clergy to set aside their wives.

During her reign, Mary Tudor acquired her nickname "Bloody Mary" due to her revenge on those that opposed her religious reforms. She imprisoned Archbishop Cranmer for annulling her mother's marriage to Henry VIII, as well as for making Protestant changes in the prayer book. Additionally, she forced him to watch from his prison cell the burning of Bishops Latimer and Nicholas Ridley. Terrified by the horrible scene he had witnessed, Bishop Cranmer denied his Protestant principles and submitted to papal authority. Nevertheless, Mary condemned him to death. On the day of his death, in March 1556, Cranmer took courage. The guards took

---

5. Ibid.

him to St. Mary's Church, where a special platform was set up. Following a sermon, they gave him the opportunity publically to recant his departure from the Catholic Church. To their surprise, he defiantly declared his Protestant faith. They then tied him to the pyre and set it burning. As the flames whipped about him, he held out his hand with which he signed his renunciation into the flames, until the fire consumed it.

In fear from Cranmer's execution, Thomas Beccon, who assisted Cranmer in the revisions to the *Book of Common Prayer*, fled to Strasbourg and then to Frankfurt. He remained there, only returning to England after Mary Tudor's death. Peter Martyr likewise fled England for Strasbourg, where they appointed him professor of theology. Sensing the danger, John Knox in 1554 fled Scotland for Frankfurt. Yet, due to his outspoken preaching, he remained there only briefly. January 1555 found him in Geneva, where he studied for three years with John Calvin. While in Geneva, Knox helped Cloverdale prepare the Geneva Bible. Following his study with Calvin, Knox left Geneva to serve as the pastor of an English refugee congregation in Frankfurt. However, due to his differences with the congregation over the conducting of the liturgy, they forced him to leave Frankfurt. To many a Protestant's relief, Mary Tudor died in 1558.

Protestant Elizabeth I, the most popular Queen

Being only three years old at the time when Henry executed her mother, Anne Boleyn, Elizabeth lived for seven additional years only recognized as the bastard daughter of Henry VIII. Nevertheless, she sought to use productively the opportunities offered to her, and she took advantage of the finest classical education of the day. She became very biblically astute through her daily reading of the New Testament in Greek. Although she did not feel deep religious convictions, she was a Protestant. Since her life was in danger during Mary Tudor's reign, as a child she wisely conformed to Mary's reinstatement of the Catholic ritual.

Elizabeth Recognized as Queen

On the morning of November 17, 1558, the Lord Chancellor in the House of Lords announced Mary Tudor's death. Nicholas Throckmorton had not waited for the official announcement, as he was on the road early that morning to carry the good news to the new queen. The earls of Arundel and Pembroke, sent by the council, soon joined him on his journey. Arriving at Hatfield shortly prior to noon, they found Elizabeth sitting under an oak tree, reading from the Greek New Testament. She stood up as they approached her. They knelt down before her and saluted her as the new queen. Elizabeth was speechless and overcome with emotions. She fell to her knees, quoting from the Latin version of Psalm 118, "This is the Lord's doing; it is marvelous in our eyes!"[6]

Elizabeth, the illegitimate daughter of Anne Boleyn and Henry VIII, and the half-sister of Mary Tudor, would serve as queen from 1558 to 1603. Of all Henry VIII's children, she most resembled him in terms of ability and popularity. As queen, Elizabeth proceeded cautiously in making changes. She chose not to be the "Supreme Head" of the church, a title that offended Catholics. Instead, she chose the title "Supreme Governor" of the Church of England. Further, the new prayer book that she approved was a revision of the less offensive prayer book that Edward VI approved. Its forms manifested an inclusive theology, which avoided theological extremes. As such, it possessed a moderate form of Calvinism in its theology, and the use of Catholic vestments such as the alb, chasuble, and cope. Further, the new 1559 *Book of Common Prayer* combined two previous formulas used during the celebration of the Lord's Supper. When the minister distributed the bread to the people, the new formula read, "The body of our Lord Jesus Christ which was given for thee preserve thy body and soul unto everlasting life. Take and eat this in remembrance that Christ died for thee and feed on Him in thy heart by faith with thanksgiving."[7] It also removed the offensive prayer, "From the Bishop of Rome and all his detestable enormities, Good Lord, deliver us."[8] The Calvinists were upset regarding the efforts to respect the diversity within the kingdom, but eventually the outcries died down. Her inclusive theological stance continued in her revision of Cranmer's 1553 Forty-Two Articles, as the 1562 Thirty-Nine Articles. Although the Thirty-Nine Articles rejected several Catholic features, it served as a doctrinal foundation on which most Protestants could agree.

Like her father, Henry VIII, Elizabeth's religious stances often came more from political rather than faith motives. Even though the Catholics remained a threat to her reign, she felt disgust for Calvinists, claiming them to be too fanatical, strait-laced, and rebellious for the good of the

6. Weir, *Children of Henry VIII*, 362–63.
7. Gonzalez, *Story of Christianity*, 2:79.
8. Price and Weil, *Liturgy for Living*, 56.

kingdom. In a political move, she affirmed the Augsburg Confession, as the Lutheran system of bishops was better suited to the royal hierarchy, even though there were few Lutherans in England. Toward the end of her reign, Catholics indicated that they could look to the pope for their spiritual direction, and to the queen in the fulfillment of their civic responsibilities. In time, based on their ability to manifest these dual loyalties, she permitted Catholics to worship openly throughout the kingdom.

The Defeat of the Spanish Armada

Since England was an island nation, Elizabeth knew that it needed to secure its international trade routes in order to import needed economic resources. Therefore, two seminal events would define her reign: the defeat of the Spanish Armada, and the exploration of the New World.

The first of these, the defeat of the Spanish Armada, began with the tangled web of Philip II of Spain seeking Elizabeth's hand in marriage, and Scotland's Mary Stuart's marriage to Francis II of France. Philip II of Spain, the widower of Elizabeth's deceased half-sister Mary Tudor, in quest of a political union between England and Spain, sought to persuade Elizabeth to marry him. Displaying great charm in the face of his advances, she avoided giving him an answer to his proposals of marriage. Yet, Elizabeth also realized that Spain was a major world power with which England competed for economic resources. She also knew that England could not afford to engage in open warfare against Spain. However, she could covertly aid militarily the rebels fighting in the Netherlands. She could also clandestinely commission a group of privateers to disrupt commerce by raiding Spanish vessels and towns. Elizabeth therefore undertook these stealthy military actions against Spain.

Meanwhile, in 1558, another member of the royal family, Mary Stuart, Queen of Scots, married the heir to the French throne, the future Francis II. Their marriage sealed a political union between Scotland and France. Due to Mary Stuart having lived in France since 1554, her mother, Mary of Lorraine, the Guise, had ruled Scotland in her behalf. In an unexpected turn of events, in 1560 Mary of Guise died. Moreover, that same year Mary Stuart's husband, King Francis II, likewise died. Thereupon, the Scottish nobles invited Mary Stuart to return to Scotland. She accepted their invitation, and in 1561 returned to Scotland. Initially following the advice of her illegitimate half-brother James Stuart, earl of Morey, the Catholic Mary Stuart was prudent and did not force changes upon Reformed Scotland. Yet, in time, she became more bold and reckless, and insisted on the celebration of the Mass. Despite John Calvin's best counsel to Knox to choose his battles, John Knox remained outspoken against the policies of Mary Stuart.

A turning point in her public support occurred when the widowed Mary Stuart married Henry Stewart, Lord Darnley, her Catholic cousin. Moray, her court advisor, opposed the marriage. Yet Mary ignored his counsel and expelled him from the court. On June 19, 1566, a son was born in Edinburgh Castle to Mary and Darnley, the future James VI of Scotland and James I of England. With his birth, Mary felt a more secure grip on the throne.

Eventually, Mary's love for Darnley soured, fueled primarily by her bitterness toward Darnley for his March 1566 murder of her Italian secretary. Moreover, in the meanwhile, she fell in love with a Protestant noble, James Hepburn, the earl of Bothwell. He was a rough man whose qualities contrasted greatly to those of her husband Darnley. In a secret plot, she moved Darnley, who was recovering from smallpox, from Glasgow to a small house on the edge of Edinburgh. Mary spent a part of his last evening with him. Early on the next morning, February 10, 1567, the house blew up, with Darnley's dead body found nearby. The authorities charged Bothwell with the murder, however, due to Mary's influence, the court did not convict him. The following May 3, Bothwell divorced his wife. Using Protestant rites, on May 15, Mary and Bothwell married. Incensed Protestants and Catholics alike turned against her, and a month later she was imprisoned. On July 24, 1567, they forced her to appoint the Protestant Morey to rule in behalf of her one-year-old son, the future James VI of Scotland. On July 26, Knox preached at the coronation of the infant king, whom they would rear as a Calvinist. In May 1568, Mary Tudor escaped from prison, and fled for refuge to her cousin Queen Elizabeth. Elizabeth did not receive her cousin warmly, yet she treated her with the respect deserved of a queen of Scotland. However, when there was an attempt on Elizabeth's life, she had enough of Mary's ambition and imprisoned her. Later, on February 8, 1587, the Privy Council beheaded Mary in the Tower of London.

Mary's execution incensed Philip II of Spain, as it ended his hopes of placing a Catholic king upon the Scottish throne. In addition, his lingering anger concerning Elizabeth's spurring of his marital advances, and her commissioning of English privateers to raid Spanish towns and ships, made him even more determined to overthrow the English queen. He thus planned for his Spanish Armada to transport Spanish troops from the Netherlands in an invasion of the English homeland. However, he poorly planned and ineffectively executed his invasion. Aware of the forthcoming invasion, in 1588 Elizabeth called back her privateers from raiding Spanish vessels and towns, for their use in the defense of the homeland. When the large, unwieldy vessels of the Spanish Armada reached English waters, they faced the smaller, faster, more maneuverable privateer vessels fitted with superior cannons. In addition, the privateers developed new battle tactics in their skirmishes with Spanish ships.

Even though damaged by the superior English tactics, an overwhelming number of Spanish ships sailed into open waters on their way to the Netherlands. Upon reaching the Netherlands, the Spanish captains discovered that the admiralty failed to calculate that their ships' drafts were too deep to enter the harbors, and no small boats were provided to ferry the troops to the ships. The Spanish captains thereupon decided to return home. In order to avoid sailing again through the English Channel, they sailed around Scotland and Ireland. Both navigational errors and a terrible storm in the North Atlantic brought the ships too close to the coast. The result was that the strong winds drove many of their ships onto the rocks in Ireland. Because of these errors, more men died as the result of storm, starvation, and disease than died in the sea battle. In the defeat of the Spanish Armada, the English lost fifty to one hundred sailors, and yet no ships were lost. However, after their victory at sea, some 6,000 to 8,000 English sailors died from typhus and dysentery. Due to the dismal financial situation, the English government compounded their misery by discharging many of the sailors from the service without pay. The crown's neglect of these sailors contrasted with the financial assistance that Spanish government gave to its survivors. In all, the Spanish lost 5,000 men and half of its fleet during its voyage. Yet many more men died from diseases back in Spain than injuries at sea. The defeat of the Spanish Armada eliminated the last significant threat to Elizabeth's throne.

The Exploration of the New World

Long before Queen Elizabeth's reign, the major world powers expressed an interest in world exploration. Under a charter granted by King Henry VII, Captain John Cabot discovered North America, giving England its first claim in the New World. Most likely, he reached Nova Scotia or Labrador.

In 1524, the French-supported Florentine navigator Giovanni de Verrazano sailed up the North American eastern coast, mapping coastal North Carolina and New England. In 1582, mapmakers translated his work into English. In addition, in 1526 the Spanish adventurer Luis Vasquez de Ayllon sailed up North Carolina's Cape Fear River. However, he abandoned his attempts at establishing a colony due to illnesses, insufficient supplies, and the threat of mutiny. Likewise, in 1561 Angel de Villafane sailed from Vera Cruz to Hatteras, but was unable to surmount the challenges posed by the coastal barrier islands.

Despite French and Spanish exploration from 1524 to 1561, almost a century would pass before there would be additional English exploration of North America. Nevertheless, Elizabeth moved swiftly to make economic and social changes to strengthen the nation. Recovering from the effects of the Black Death, the urban areas such as London had reached 100,000 inhabitants. They needed to import resources from throughout the world in order to feed their growing populace, and to fuel their emerging economic engines. With that goal in mind, in March of 1584 Elizabeth granted a charter to Sir Walter Raleigh to establish an English colony in America. Soon afterwards, Raleigh commissioned Captains Philip Armadas and Arthur Barlowe to explore the new world and to find a suitable place for colonization. On July 2, after sailing for sixty-seven days, they reached the shores of North Carolina, to an island within the Pamlico Sound the natives called Roanoke. On their return, the captains' glowing reports to Raleigh of available resources in the new land excited the royal court. As a result, the queen knighted Sir Walter Raleigh, and named the land "Virginia" after the unmarried Queen Elizabeth.

In April 1585, under the command of Richard Greenville, 108 men on seven ships sailed from Plymouth, England. Referred to as the "Ralph Lane Colony" after one of their leaders, they included a number of men that lacked the needed skills for settling in the New World. On August 17, they arrived at Roanoke Island, and built "Fort Raleigh." However, this venture was unsuccessful due to conflict among the leadership, wasted time seeking gold in an inland waterway, increased hostility between the settlers and the Native Americans, and the lack of planning. Meanwhile, Richard Greenville sailed for England to secure additional provisions. Yet, due to renewed hostility with some of the Native Americans, and faced with starvation, the settlers were relieved to see Sir Francis Drake's fleet off the coast. In 1586, loaned a ship by Drake, they sailed to England. Within a month of their departure for England, Sir Richard Greenville's three supply ships arrived off the North Carolina coast. After searching in vain for the "Lane Colony," Greenville left fifteen men with two years' supplies to maintain England's legal claim on North America.

Upon the Lane Colony's return to England, Sir Walter Raleigh organized a new colonization attempt known as the "John White Colony." Sailing in May 1587, this second attempt by 120 settlers included 17 women and nine children. Arriving off Hatteras Island in late July 1587, they continued to Roanoke Island. Finding Fort Raleigh in ruins, and no sign of the men that Sir Richard Greenville left, Fernandez, one of the major investors in the venture, decided not to take his ships onward to the Chesapeake Bay. The settlers, however, decided to remain at Roanoke Island, rebuild the fort, and repair the housing. Landing ashore in mid-summer, the settlers missed the opportunity to plant crops that they could harvest by winter. Further, the coastal Algonquin tribe was hostile to the English settlers. The colonists needing supplies for the winter, John White, in late August 1587, returned to England. Before sailing, the settlers told him that, for safety reasons, they were planning to move inland about fifty miles. They promised to leave a sign indicating their new location, along with a sign if the colony was in peril. On arriving in England in November 1587, John White found all of England prepared for the invasion of the Spanish Armada. Finally reaching Roanoke Island in August 1590, he found no signs of the colony, other than a few broken pieces of armor, his chests buried on the sandy beach containing his personal items, and the word "Croatoan" carved on a tree. The fate of the "Lost Colony" is a mystery to this day.

The failed investments in Sir Walter Raleigh's attempts to colonize America, and the repelling of the Spanish Armada, financially strained the royal treasury. The crown decided that future ventures should be a cooperative effort between the merchant community and the government. Elizabeth died on March 24, 1603, surrounded by vestiges of her New World explorations. Elizabeth never lived to see the fulfillment of her dream of a permanent English settlement in America. That dream came to fulfillment in 1607 in the establishment of a new colony in Virginia. The new colony's name was Jamestown, after her successor to the throne, James I.

The Reformation in Scotland

No one knows the origin of Christianity in Scotland. History simply records that Columba was the first known Christian leader in Scotland. He arrived in Scotland from Ireland in 563. He established a church on Iona, an island on the western coast. The Celtic cross often found in some sanctuaries today are copies of the Celtic cross found near the Iona abbey.

The Culdees (Servants or Friends of God), a group of monks, likewise established an abbey on the eastern Scottish coast. They followed the example of Saint Andrew (Saint Peter's brother) as their patron saint. The missionary work of Saint Columba and that of the Culdees preceded any missionary work by the Roman Catholic Church. In time, these first Scottish Christians adopted the name of the Old Celtic Church. Eventually, their church's headquarters relocated to Saint Andrews on the eastern coastal plain. From its seaports at Saint Andrews, Presbyterians sailed to the uttermost parts of the earth, carrying the gospel message with them.

Beginning in 1150, Margaret, the wife of the Scottish King Malcolm III, as well as her sons, who became kings of Scotland, sought transform the Old Celtic Church into a low church form of the Roman Catholic Church. At the same time, the church never provided for reform to better the lives of the common people. Because of the neglect, the common people yearned for strong leadership. In time, several leaders stepped forward, shining a light of hope in the midst of the darkness. Patrick Hamilton boldly preached the Reformed faith. Sadly, however, due to the successes of his reforms, the Roman Catholic archbishop tried him and burned him at the stake in late February 1528.

During the sixteenth century, Scotland was a land composed of two different languages and cultures—Lowland English and Highland Gaelic. The Lowland Scots were highly influenced by their northern English neighbors, who were more financially prosperous. In contrast, the Highlanders, governed by a gathering of the clans, took their surnames from the clan chiefs. The Protestant clans recognized the fourth and fifth earls of Argyll (both named Archibald Campbell) as the mediators between the northern Gaelic Highland clans and the English-speaking Lowlanders. Gaelic was an oral language, detached from the print culture that had characterized much of the Reformation movement. In order to secure Gaelic texts of reformation writings, during the 1500s, the earl of Argyll secured the services of the notary John Carswell. He named him the superintendent of Argyll and the bishop of the Isles. Carswell published a free translation of the Kirk's *Book of Common Order*, and a version of Calvin's small catechism.

John Knox and the Scottish Reformation Movement

The Early Years

Knox was a Lowland Scot, born between 1503 and 1515, with 1514 being the most likely date. His father, William Knox, and his grandfather were hard working tenant farmers on the East Lothian estate of the earl of Bothwell. His mother was descended from the Sinclair clan. Some scholars suggest that during September 1513 his father died at the Battle of Flodden. If so, either John Knox was an infant at his father's death, or he was born after his father's death. John Knox was the younger of two boys, the elder brother bearing his father's name, William. While John Knox was a child, his mother likewise died.

At fifteen years old, John Knox entered St. Andrews to study toward the priesthood. Following two years of study in the arts, the university granted him at Bachelor of Arts degree. He continued his studies under John Major, one of the greatest scholars of the time. The works of the martyred Patrick Hamilton and the preaching of George Wishart greatly influenced him. Following three to four years of advanced studies, the university likewise granted John Knox a Bachelor of Divinity. Knox was an outstanding student at the university. Upon his ordination to the priesthood on Easter Eve, 1536, instead of seeking an appointment to a parish, he became the tutor of two young children. In the meanwhile, he maintained close contact with George Wishart. Wishart, once a schoolmaster at Montrose, was declared by the church a heretic because of his teaching Greek in grammar school. In fear for his life, he carried with him a two-edged longsword. Whenever Wishart preached in Lothian, John Knox carried Wishart's sword for him and served as his bodyguard.

John Knox Taken Prisoner and Serves on Slave Galley

In December 1545, on Cardinal Beaton's orders, Catholic supporters seized George Wishart and took him as a prisoner to St. Andrews Castle. In March 1546, they executed him. Two months later, in revenge for his execution, five men forced their way into St. Andrews Castle. They captured the archbishop, Cardinal Beaton, executed him, and hung his body from the castle walls. The father of the two boys whom Knox tutored was among the men who seized the castle. After Protestant forces took the castle, the father instructed Knox to bring his two sons to him at the castle. Following his safe delivery of the boys, Knox planned to leave for Germany. However, once within the castle, they made Knox the chaplain of the castle's Protestant community. The garrison within the castle, weakened by an outbreak of the bubonic plague and constant artillery shelling, was doomed. Sent by Mary of Guise, the regent of Scotland, French troops stormed the castle, and took John Knox and others as prisoners.

For nineteen months, John Knox served as a galley slave. Being top-heavy, the galley slave ships sailed only during the summer months. Their mission was to ferry soldiers and supplies to Scotland, and to intercept English ships seeking to supply the Scottish Reformation party. The vessels were massive in size, at 150 long, and with a beam of 50 feet. Each ship's complement consisted of 100 naval crewmembers, along with 300 slaves as rowers. Each side of the ship had 25 rows, each row manned by six slaves. Chained together night and day, the men suffered from the effects of the blazing sun to the cold and freezing rain. At night, they slept on straw mats beneath their bench. Rats abounded on the ships, some of them carrying the bubonic plague. Understandably, during his imprisonment, Knox suffered from severe health problems, and his companions feared that he would die from the hard labor and living conditions. His health broken, after John Knox completed his sentence, the Scottish crown released him. He returned to England, where the court appointed him as one of the six court chaplains to the child king, Edward VI. While there, he met and married his first wife, the English Marjorie Bowes. Her family strongly opposed her marriage to Knox.

John Knox Returns to Scotland

Later, John Knox, now a notary and a Reformed preacher, desired to return to Edinburgh, Scotland. Elizabeth intentionally delayed granting his passport due to her dislike of his earlier pamphlet, "The First Blast of the Trumpet against the Monstrous Regiment of Women." John Knox wrote the pamphlet in protest against her half-sister Mary Tudor, but Elizabeth sensed that Knox generally felt prejudice against women monarchs. After considerable delay, in 1559 she granted him a passport. Two days after his arrival in Scotland, Elizabeth declared him an outlaw. She summoned him to appear in Stirling for his trial. Fearing execution, he went to Perth, a walled town that his supporters could defend. In Perth, he preached at the Church of St. John the Baptist. His sermon so inflamed the congregation that they responded by looting the church, attacking two friaries in the town, taking their silver, and breaking their images. Afterwards, Knox traveled to St. Andrews. Once again, he preached a sermon to which the congregation responded by vandalizing and looting the sanctuary.

In August 1560, the Scottish Parliament adopted the Reformed faith as the official system of doctrinal belief. It approved a worship book modeled after Calvin's *La Forme des Prieres*, along with the Scots Confession as its doctrinal statement. Despite Knox's request that the Lord's Supper to be celebrated monthly, due to the shortage of ministers, they reduced the requirement to four times a year. Parliament further stated that both the Old Testament and the New Testament were to be read during worship, and that the entire service was to be conducted from the pulpit so that all persons might be able clearly to hear the minister's voice.

In December 1560, the first General Assembly of the Church of Scotland met with six ministers and thirty-five ruling elders. Under John Knox's guidance, they prepared a *Book of Church Order*, which included provisions for congregations to elect elders for one year, and to institute the office of regional superintendent. In addition, within every church was a public school, with a school master teaching Latin, grammar, and catechism. The church likewise provided scholarships in order that poor children might attend these schools.

Knox's Marriage and Illness

Tragically, in December 1560, after eight years of marriage, Knox's wife, Marjorie, died. No more than twenty-five years old at the time, her cause of death remains unknown. Her demise left John to care for his two sons, Nathaniel and Eleazar, ages three and a-half and two years old. John Calvin, whose own wife died in 1549, wrote Knox a letter of condolence over his loss. Marjorie's mother, Mrs. Bowes, came to stay with Knox and the boys, in order to assist him in their rearing. She returned home to England four years later, following John Knox's marriage on Palm Sunday 1564 to Margaret Stewart, the daughter of an old friend, Andrew Stewart, and a distant cousin of the queen. At the time of his second marriage, John Knox was nearly fifty years of age, while the bride was seventeen. They had three daughters, Martha, Margaret, and Elizabeth, who would be six, four, and two years old when their father died.

John Knox suffered from many of the same physical ailments as did many of the other Reformers. In October 1570, he suffered a stroke, probably caused by a cerebral thrombosis. As a result, he had to restrict his preaching engagements. Yet he continued faithfully to serve his congregation. Six weeks prior to Knox's death, Sir Henry Killigrew, the English ambassador to the Scottish court, worshipped at St. Giles. Following worship, he wrote these comments: "John Knox is now so feeble as scare he can stand alone, or speak to be heard of any audience; yet doth he every Sunday cause himself to be carried to a place where certain numbers do hear him and doth preach with the same vehemence and zeal that he ever did."[9]

On November 9, 1572, Knox preached his last sermon and performed his last pastoral duties. Two days later, after a severe coughing spasm, Knox coughed up a great amount of phlegm. The following Tuesday, he found himself unable to read the Bible. Therefore, others daily read to him. On Friday, he was confused, thinking that he was to preach that day at St. Giles. On Monday, the Kirk Session visited with him and noted that he seemed to be short of breath. That following Friday, November 21, he asked for the ordering of his wooden coffin. Knox rallied the next day and entertained friends at supper. However, on Sunday, he had difficulty breathing and it was evident that death was soon. On Monday, November 24, at about ten in the morning, again he rallied, dressed, and sat in a chair for about half an hour. That same day, at five in the afternoon, John Knox asked his wife to read to him from 1 Corinthians 15 and John 17. Afterwards, he fell into a deep sleep. At about eleven in the evening, he gave a deep sigh, suddenly exclaimed, "Now it is come," and breathed his last.[10] Most likely, John Knox died of a lower respiratory tract infection, probably bronchopneumonia.

The church buried John Knox on Wednesday, November 26, in the St. Giles Church graveyard. In 1633, the government erected the Parliament house and other buildings over the site. Currently, a marking designating John Knox's grave is set at parking space number twenty-three, near the St. Giles Church. As James Douglas, the newly elected fourth earl of Morton, stood by John Knox's grave, he declared, "Here lies one who never feared

---

9. Wilkinson, *Medical History of the Reformers*, 106.

10. Ibid., 108–9.

nor flattered any flesh."[11] Following Knox's death, his family had few financial resources. The regent, Lord Morton, asked the General Assembly to continue paying his ministerial stipend to his widow for one year after his death. John Knox's life has influenced not only the birth of Presbyterianism, but also the character of the Scottish peoples.

James I unites England and Scotland under One Throne

James VI, King of Scotland, was the son of Mary Stuart, "Queen of Scots," and Henry Stewart, the Lord Darnley, as well as the grandson of James V and Mary of Guise. He reined over Scotland as king from 1567 to 1603, prior to his reign over both Scotland and England, from 1603 to 1625. Being a small child at the time of his royal coronation, the council appointed the Protestant Morton to be his regent, to administer the kingdom on his behalf. Morton, a pragmatist, understood the importance of maintaining the episcopate in order to keep control of the church's historic properties.

At James' 1603 coronation as king of England and Scotland, all the various religious parties looked favorably upon him. The Catholics hoped that his rule would manifest the legacy of his Catholic mother Mary, Queen of Scots. The Presbyterians saw favor due to his Calvinistic education at the hands of Lord Morey, the illegitimate son of King James V and Lady Margaret Erskine. The Anglicans saw favor in his disdain for the Presbyterian form of representative government.

In 1541, Andrew Melville, a Scottish Protestant leader, concerned that the Catholic Scottish King James VI would expand the power of the Scottish bishops over Presbyterians, convinced the Scottish General Assembly to approve the *Second Book of Discipline*. The new book explicitly stated that the ecclesiastical powers of church discipline lay within the jurisdiction of the presbyteries, not the bishop. James VI would not submit to this challenge to his authority. Therefore, in 1591 he asserted his royal power, maintaining that he alone possessed the right to call into session the General Assembly. He exiled Melville and the other Presbyterians who supported strengthening the judicial powers of the presbyteries. Further, in seeking to undermine the presbytery's powers, James created two high commissions to hear and to administer all church court cases arising within the presbyteries. An archbishop headed each high commission. Likewise, James insisted that due to apostolic succession the bishops retained the authority

11. Ibid.,108.

of confirmation. Finally, James forced the Church of Scotland's General Assembly to approve several Roman Catholic liturgical characteristics: all worshippers to kneel during the celebration of the Lord's Supper, permission granted for the observance of private baptisms and celebrations of the Lord's Supper, and all the Scots required to observe the church calendar.

In addition, the 1604 (English and Scottish) Jacobean prayer book added a rubric specifying that only a "lawful minister" could perform baptisms, eliminating the provisions for emergency baptisms. The more significant eucharistic changes came in the 1662 *Book of Common Prayer*, with the introduction of a rubric that allowed the priest during the service to place on the table the bread and the wine. This change reversed the former rubric in Edward VI's 1552 *Book of Common Prayer*, which required the bread and wine to be placed on the table prior to the service. As the 1662 *Book of Common Prayer* was the first prayer book issued following the printing of the King James Bible, the Epistle and Gospel readings were from the King James translation. However, the 1662 prayer book retained the Psalter readings from the Great Bible translation. Miles Coverdale's Great Bible translation of the Psalter endures to this day.

The Puritan Movement

Early during James' reign, John Smyth, a former Anglican clergyman, developed an affinity with the doctrinal beliefs of those congregations separating themselves from the Church of England. In time, he became the pastor of a congregation in Gainsborough, which was in sympathy with his feelings. Other congregations soon followed in withdrawal from the Church of England. Meeting opposition within their communities, in 1608 to 1609 they moved to Amsterdam, and founded their first congregation on Dutch soil. John Smyth and his followers rejected strict Calvinism. Instead, they accepted the Armenian belief that Christ died for all persons. Smyth's congregation eventually affiliated with the Dutch Mennonites. In 1611 to 1612, some of the believers returned to England under the leadership of Thomas Helwys and John Morton. In 1612, they established in London the first General Baptist congregation on English soil. People particularly appreciated both their religious toleration and their desire for separation of church and state.

During these same years, under the leadership of Henry Jacobs, William Ames, and William Bradshaw, the Puritan movement began to take root. In 1616, they established the first Congregationalist congregation at Southwick, England. Soon the English Baptist leaders asserted that Christ died only for the elect, and that believer's baptism was the only biblically accepted form of baptism. They thus initiated a second form of the Baptist faith, calling themselves the "Particular" or "Calvinistic Baptist." By 1641, believers' baptism by immersion became the standard baptismal practice for Baptists.

The Puritan movement communicated its doctrinal beliefs through preaching, rather than the liturgy of the *Book of Common Prayer*. Thus, the Puritan congregations built their sanctuaries to communicate their priorities in worship. Their new sanctuary design stood in sharp contrast with the traditional Anglican design. In the great Anglican cathedrals, the sanctuary would have a split chancel, the pulpit to one side of the chancel area, with a lectern located on the other side. Behind the pulpit and lectern, in the center of the chancel, was a large elevated altar. The purpose of the chancel arrangement was to draw worshippers' eyes to the altar and to the celebration of the Eucharist. In contrast, the focus of the Puritan sanctuary was upon the centered elevated pulpit with an open Bible resting upon it. The pulpit and Bible thereby replaced the Anglican altar as being the center of focus. Some sanctuaries hung a "sounding board" over the pulpit, a primitive device for acoustically projecting the spoken voice.

Frequently the Puritans were the most highly educated people within the villages. They preached extended sermons, and wrote numerous volumes commenting on the Scriptures. Appreciating the value of education, they founded Emmanuel College at Cambridge University. Every newly enrolled student in this Puritan institution of higher education would memorize, in Latin, William Ames's *The Marrow of Theology*.

The Congregationalist congregation at Leyden, in 1620, sent church members to establish a new colony in America. Under the leadership of Elder William Brewster, these pilgrims crossed the Atlantic Ocean on the Mayflower, establishing on December 21 the Plymouth Colony. Due to continued oppression under King Charles I, a number of additional Puritans later would migrate to Massachusetts. In 1621, the king granted a royal charter for the colony of Massachusetts. In 1630, pilgrims led by John Winthrop established the Massachusetts Bay Colony. In 1636, Thomas Hooker led a group from Massachusetts to found the new colony of Connecticut. Famous New England Puritans included the father-and-son team of Increase Mather (1639–1723) and Cotton Mather (1663–1728), John

Cotton (1585–1652), the poet Anne Bradstreet (1612–1672), and Jonathan Edwards (1703–1758).

Charles I and his insistence on conformity

In 1625, Charles I succeeded James I to the united throne. In 1633, Charles appointed his friend William Laud as the archbishop of Canterbury. There soon erupted continued conflicts between Charles and Parliament. At one point in the conflict, Charles stormed into the chamber of the House of Commons and demanded the arrest of several of its members. (Because of his irregular actions that day, the English king or queen remains restricted from entering the House of Commons.) Charles insisted that he had the royal right to imprison someone without charging them of a crime, the right to tax without Parliament's approval, and to enact religious reforms that would force Presbyterians and Puritans to worship as Anglicans. On July 23, 1637, Charles ordered all congregations to conform to a version of the previous unpopular 1549 *Book of Common Prayer*. That order infuriated the Scottish Presbyterians, and aroused great opposition. On the day of implementation, the dean of Edinburgh read from the 1549 *Book of Common Prayer* in John Knox's former St. Giles Church, whereupon Jenny Geddes, a Scottish maid, hurled at the minister the little stool upon which she sat. He quickly ducked the missile that she threw at him. The whole congregation soon joined her means of protest, throwing their own stools at the retreating ministers. Not wanting to suffer the same fate, Bishop Walter Whitford led a service in the cathedral church at Brechin armed with two loaded pistols. There was no mention of any disturbance during the service that morning! Finally, in February 28, 1638, in the Greyfriar's churchyard, the Scottish Presbyterians bound themselves together in the National Covenant, in which they pledged to defend Presbyterianism with their very lives. Today, members of the Associate Reformed Presbyterian denomination are the descendants of those 1638 Covenanters.

The Short and the Long Parliaments

Angered at the Scots' resistance to his reforms, Charles was more determined to enforce his orders. As a result, a war broke out between the Scottish and English forces. To pay for the expenses for his war, in April 1640 Charles summoned the English Parliament into meeting. After coming to order, however, it was apparent that old grievances surfaced against the king. He quickly dissolved the "Short Parliament." In the meanwhile, the Scottish forces invaded England. Charles needed money to support his army. Desperate, the king called the "Long Parliament" into session in November 1640. The Puritans were in the majority. They imprisoned Bishop William Laud and they abolished the powers of the high commission to administer church judicial cases. In 1642, in an act of desperation, King Charles tried to kidnap family members of unsupportive representatives in the House of Commons. Doing so finally led to the outbreak of a civil war.

The Puritan Response in the Westminster Confession of Faith

One of the most lasting effects of the Long Parliament was the 1643 decision to abolish the Episcopal form of church government, and to call for an assembly of 121 clergy and 31 laity to advise Parliament in regards to the religious differences within the kingdom. The Assembly met July 1, 1643, in Westminster Cathedral. Among their achievements, the Westminster Assembly wrote the Westminster Confession of Faith and Catechisms, as well as a Directory for Worship to replace the *Book of Common Prayer*. In the Directory for Worship, the Westminster divines embraced a middle way between the conformity of episcopacy and the lack of standardized liturgical patterns in congregationalism. In 1647, the Westminster divines presented the Westminster Confession of Faith, with scriptural proofs that Parliament, and later the Church of Scotland, adopted. Further, Parliament and the Church of Scotland approved a longer and a shorter catechism. The Westminster Assembly's last recorded meeting was on February 22, 1649. In all, they met for five and a half years, on average meeting four times a week.

Oliver Cromwell and the Rump Parliament

While the Westminster Assembly met, the civil war continued. On July 2, 1644, the army led by Oliver Cromwell, a member of Parliament, defeated the king's army on Marston Moor near York. On June 14, 1645, Cromwell's army once again defeated King Charles' army near Naseby. The rebels, in capturing the camp of the king's forces, discovered evidence that Charles encouraged foreign forces to support his cause. The following year, Charles surrendered to Scottish forces and asked for mercy. The Scottish forces turned him over to the English Parliament for trial.

Parliament's forces, having defeated the army, demanded political toleration of the nation's religious diversity. The rigid Calvinistic Presbyterianism of the old parliamentary majority was not in step with the more tolerant attitudes of the troops. Tensions grew between Parliament and Cromwell's army, leading to Parliament's consideration of dissolving the army. Meanwhile, King Charles escaped from his imprisonment, and promised to support the establishment of Presbyterianism in England as well as Scotland. As a result, many of the Presbyterian Scots supported him, and thereupon they invaded England. In August 1648, Oliver Cromwell's army scattered the Scots; followed by the December 1648 Pride's Purge, which expelled from Parliament the Presbyterian members. Parliament's enemies thereafter referred to it as a "Rump Parliament." The Rump Parliament initiated charges of treason against Charles. On January 30, 1649, despite the House of Lords' objection, the House of Commons of Parliament executed Charles for treason.

The Parliament then installed Oliver Cromwell as "Lord Protector." He served as the national leader for the next eleven years. Parliament's army would conquer Catholic Ireland in 1649, and Scotland in 1650. Soon, following Cromwell's death in September 1658, old religious conflicts again reared their heads.

The Commonwealth Changed the English Church

Yet, the establishment of the Commonwealth had changed England. No longer did the established church and government have the same significant influence over the lives of the subjects. Separatist groups gained political influence within the halls of power. As a result, the government became more tolerant of religious diversity within the realm. Roman Catholics found less persecution from newer monarchies. Anglicans began to integrate into the upper socioeconomic classes, along with the Roman Catholics. As "Lord Protector," Cromwell permitted the Jews, previously expelled in 1290, to return to England. Moreover, the church established a more Presbyterian form of polity, with no hierarchy, except for a London committee known as the "Triers" to examine ministerial candidates. Some congregations formed presbyteries to offer mutual accountability and support. Parishes could choose between using the Westminster Directory for Worship or the *Book of Common Prayer*. Interestingly, the Westminster Directory for Worship stated that during worship a full chapter of the Old and New Testaments be read in continuous order. The inclusion of reading both testaments differed from the practice of Bucer and Calvin, who only insisted only on one reading from Scripture. Further, the manner of receiving the Lord's Supper they left to the discretion of the parish, so that the English Puritans might receive the elements sitting in their pews, and the Scots could receive them at the table. The Puritans particularly liked the members to partake of the elements at the same time, and to serve the elements to one another.

The great diversity in church order and worship ended in 1660 with Parliament's restoration of Charles II as king, and his implementation of Anglican polity and the use of the *Book of Common Prayer*. Further, Charles punished those who signed his royal predecessor's death warrant, putting nine of them to death. He likewise exhumed Oliver Cromwell's body from its burial place in Westminster Abby, and buried it in a common pit. Nevertheless, overall, Charles II pursued policies that exhibited tolerance and power sharing with Parliament. Obviously, he did not want to make the same political mistakes as had Charles I. Charles II died in 1685, at the last moment converting to Roman Catholicism.

The Reformation Movement in Ireland and Wales

In Ireland, although the Reformation movement made major inroads with the upper socioeconomic classes, it never displaced loyalty toward the Catholic Church among the common people. The failure was due to the actions of the later members of the Tudor dynasty, in attempting to establish within Ireland a feudal English medieval society. In addition, the royal exploitation of the people and their resources created a lasting resentment among the masses. The Catholic Church identified with the Irish resistance to English exploitation. Queen Elizabeth promoted the implementation of plantation settlements. These new settlements resulted in major Irish wars in the 1570s and 1590s. In an effort to promote the Protestant faith, Queen Elizabeth commissioned John Kearny, a Cambridge-educated clergyman, to publish in 1571 a Protestant catechism and alphabet in Gaelic. In 1609, James I established the Ulster Plantation, importing to Ireland defiant Presbyterians from the English-Scottish border. A number of these imported Presbyterians were not diligent Presbyterians, but they were willing to claim the faith in order to seize land from Irish Catholics. Understandably, the Irish translated the Gaelic word for Protestant as "Scotsman" or "Englishman"!

Wales, in contrast to Ireland, made a smoother transition. The Tudors by heritage were Welch princes, and therefore were far more sensitive to the cultural interests of the Welch. They established Jesus College in Oxford University, which helped to cement the support of the social elite, as well as to provide a training ground for Protestant clergy and future political leaders. In 1588, a Cambridge-educated Welch clergyman, William Morgan, completed a translation of the Bible into Welsh. Others likewise translated into Welsh the English *Book of Common Prayer*. As a result, the Catholic faith rapidly declined among the populace.

6

The Reformation in the Netherlands and France

The Dutch Reformation

As the birthplace of the Brethren of Common Life and Erasmus of Rotterdam, reform within the Low Countries congregations preceded the Protestant Reformation. In subsequent years, Lutheran and Anabaptist ministers began missionary work throughout the country. Later, Calvinist missionaries came from Geneva, France, and southern Germany. In response, Charles V, the Holy Roman Emperor, issued edicts prohibiting Protestant preaching, especially that performed by the Anabaptists. As a result, the authorities executed the Anabaptists by the tens of thousands. Nevertheless, Charles was popular with most of the people, who considered the Protestants as heretics. Nevertheless, Protestantism continued to grow among the peoples, especially Calvinism.

The Ascension of Philip II to the Throne

In 1555, with the ascension of Philip II to the throne of the Netherlands, attitudes began to change. Whereas Charles spoke Flemish and understood the independent culture of the Netherlands, Philip did not. Further, Philip felt that God appointed him to rid his entire realm of Protestants. The next thirty years therefore were difficult times for Protestants. Within a year of the Dutch demonstrations and the 1556 sacking of churches, Philip sent the duke of Alva and his army to smash the rebellion. Catholics and Protestants condemned the brutality. William of Orange progressively reared a

Lutheran, then a nominal Catholic, and finally a Calvinist—successfully led Calvinistic military forces against the duke of Alva.

As the result of the conflict, the Netherlands divided into seven northern Protestant provinces that retained the name the Netherlands. The remaining ten southern Catholic provinces adopted the name Belgium. As the monarchs of the Netherlands, William III, Prince of Orange, was a devout Calvinist, while his wife, Mary, was a devout Anglican. On their ascension to the throne, toleration of religious diversity became the norm within the kingdom. In 1575, William established the University of Leyden, which became highly recognized in the fields of science and theology. Calvinism, however, never became the state church, due to the north's fear of the establishment of a state church. Following William of Orange's 1577 grant of the right of freedom of worship to the Anabaptists, the Netherlands became a sanctuary for the religious oppressed. Further, many in the lower socioeconomic class moved their religious affiliation from Lutheranism to the Anabaptist religious movement. Among the Reformation voices, Zwingli's advocates attracted the middle socioeconomic class. The upper-class nobility never committed to the Reformation movement.

Religious Conflict and TULIP

Under Zwingli's influence, worshippers removed images from their sanctuaries. In 1566, in Flanders, Zwingli supporters sacked over four hundred churches. Yet, in general, religious views in the Netherlands tended toward a low-key style of reformation. As a result, Catholics, Lutherans, Anabaptists, and Reformed Protestants lived together in peace. In the late 1550s, a growing militancy developed among the Protestants, as Calvinist refugees migrated from France. By 1559, there were enough Calvinists in the Netherlands to organize a synod. In 1562, the Calvinists wrote the Belgic Confession. A series of conflicts developed between England and Spain, with Dutch involvement. These conflicts resulted in a twelve-year truce between the warring parties. During that truce, the Dutch Reformed Church made some theological decisions that would have a long-term effect upon the Reformed faith.

Arminius, a Genevan-trained Dutch theologian, supported by some government officials, challenged the Dutch Reformed Church's doctrinal standards. He argued for an inclusive form of Calvinism. In 1610 Johan Wtenbogaert became the heir of the movement, following the death of

The Reformation in the Netherlands and France

Arminius a year earlier. Wtenbogaert presented a protest to the Reformed Church's view on predestination. Concerned over his perception of the Calvinistic neglect of the freedom of human will, Wtenbogaert taught that people could reject God's gift of salvation. He arranged his assertions around five points:

1. Original sin had not so corrupted the human will that people could not respond to God's grace.
2. Human beings are able to accept or reject God's offer of salvation.
3. Baptized Christians can choose to reject God's love and thereby lose their salvation.
4. God has chosen persons for salvation due to some goodness dwelling within them, not because of God's arbitrary will.
5. Christ's death paid for the sins of every person, not just those persons who are the elect.

Franciscus Gormorus, a Dutch theologian and professor at Leiden, led the Reformed Church's response to these assertions. Using the acrostic TULIP, in which the first letter in the acrostic expresses one doctrine point, they made the following five Calvinistic assertions:

1. Total Depravity: Sin affects every area of our lives, so that through our own efforts we cannot respond to God's grace.
2. Unconditional Election: God elects some people to salvation solely based on God's own will, not because of any human spark of goodness.
3. Limited Atonement: Although Christ's death was sufficient to cover the sins of the entire world, in practice, Christ only died for the elect.
4. Irresistible Grace: Whenever God elects a person to salvation, the Holy Spirit works within that person's life to enable that one to respond in faith.
5. Perseverance of the Saints: When God elects someone for salvation, God's grace keeps that person from falling from God's salvation. The Synod of Dort (1618-1619) approved the TULIP doctrines. Even though John Calvin did not emphasize predestination as did TULIP, nevertheless, people incorrectly referred to the TULIP doctrines as the "Five Points of Calvinism." The Canons of Dort, and TULIP, became

the foundational documents of the Dutch Reformed Church, and has had a major influence on Calvinistic thinking throughout the world.

The Reformation in France

France and the Roman Catholic Church had an intertwined relationship. The kings claimed to be descended from Clovis, the first barbarian king to accept Christianity. The pope authorized that, even though the kings were not ordained, they could administer the Eucharist at their coronation. The king likewise claimed to possess magical healing powers. The University of Paris, and the Sorbonne, where a number of the Reformers studied, were conservative in their approach, and well within the Catholic theological fold. Among the masses, superstition reigned and many saw Protestantism as a manifestation of the coming of the Antichrist.

Royal politics thus would shape the development of Protestantism within France. In 1559, Henry II, the son of Francis I, died in a jousting accident. His successor was his son Francis II, who was married to Mary Queen of Scots. Quickly Mary's maternal relatives, the House of Guise, from the Loraine region, dominated his court. Being strong Catholics, they despised the Calvinistic Huguenot movement. On the December 5, 1560, upon the death of Francis II, his brother Charles IX succeeded him on the throne. At the time of his ascension, Charles IX only was ten years old. His mother, Catherine de' Medici, strengthened her son's political support by seeking reconciliation among the political factions within the kingdom. In September 1561, the Colloquy of Poissy, a meeting between Protestant and Catholic leaders, took place. The Protestant reformer Theodore Beza took part in the discussions. In January 1562, Catherine issued the Edict of January, permitting Huguenots to assembly for worship, except in walled towns. However, some Catholic political factions were unhappy with her reconciliation efforts. On March 1, 1562, in an effort to provoke a war between the Huguenots and Catholics, duke of Guise's troops attacked a Huguenot congregation in Vassy. As a result, from 1562 to 1570 the Huguenot and Catholic forces fought three savage wars, interspersed with short truces. Finally, in 1570 a peace treaty signed at Saint-Germain-en-Laye brought the promise of a lasting peace.

The Wedding that Turned Deadly

The Huguenots and the French opponents of Spanish imperialism arranged a marriage to unite two rival French political parties. At the same time, Catherine de' Medici feared the Protestant leaders gaining increased political influence. She therefore instigated a plot to assassinate Admiral Coligny, a leader among the Protestants. In setting her trap, she invited the Huguenot leaders to the August 18, 1572, wedding of Protestant Henry Bourbon and the French king's sister, Margaret of Valois. Afterwards, as Admiral Coligny returned to his lodging for the night, an assassin shot at him from a building owned by the Guise family. Coligny survived the assassination attempt, losing a finger from his right hand and sustaining a wound in his left arm. The Huguenot leaders insisted on an investigation, and the king banned the Guise family temporarily from the court.

Meanwhile, Catherine convinced the weak-willed Charles that Admiral Coligny was the leader of a Huguenot plot to overthrow his reign. As a result, on August 24, 1572, the night of St. Bartholomew's Day, with Charles and Catherine's consent, the duke of Guise targeted individuals to kill. The duke attacked Admiral Coligny, still recovering from his previous wounds. Once again, the duke severely wounded him. While he still was alive, the duke of Guise threw the admiral from his window to the street. There on the street, his body was mutilated and hanged. The king spared the lives of Louis de Condé and Henry Bourbon, due to their begging mercy and denying their Huguenot faith. The assassins that night murdered 2,000 other Huguenots. Reports claimed that blood ran down the stairs of the royal palace, the Louvre. Successive violence followed in many other parts of the kingdom. The death toll approached as many as 20,000 persons. When the pope heard the news of the massacre, he ordered the "Te Deum" sung in celebration. Yet, when Calvin heard news concerning the St. Bartholomew's Day Massacre, his grief was overwhelming. Throughout France, Protestants and Catholics alike were horrified at the violence taken against the Huguenots.

Three Henry's Vie for Power

Upon Charles IX's death, the throne passed to Charles' brother, Henry of Anjou, one of the plotters of the St. Bartholomew's Day Massacre. He would take the title of King Henry III. The war against the Protestants ended with a stalemate, granting them freedom of worship, except in Paris. However, the more radical Catholics were infuriated at the resolution of the conflict, as well as Henry's scandal-filled lifestyle. Led by Henry of Guise, they declared war on the Huguenots. Spain and Henry III would join with them in that war. In the struggle, neither side had the strength to overcome the other.

In an unexpected twist of fate, Henry II and Catherine de' Medici's youngest son died, leaving no heir. Henry III likewise did not have any heirs. Therefore, Henry Bourbon, whose life Charles IX spared in the St. Bartholomew's Day Massacre, was the rightful heir to the throne. Having escaped in 1576 from a Paris prison, he became one of the Protestant leaders. However, the Catholics would not tolerate a Protestant on the French throne. Thus, they discovered a fraudulent document that claimed that Henry, the duke of Guise, was a direct descendant of Charlemagne. Being a direct descendant of Charlemagne, Henry of Guise's claim to the French throne trumped all the rest of the contenders. Upon capturing Paris, Henry of Guise proclaimed himself as the French king.

In summary, there were three factions vying for power, each one led by a Henry: Henry III, Henry of Guise, and Henry Bourbon. On December 23, 1588, Henry III undertook to see Henry of Guise murdered, at the same place where, fifteen years earlier, he gave Henry of Guise orders to carry out the St. Bartholomew's Day Massacre. However, due to Catholic mistrust of him, Henry III fled from Paris to the safety of Henry Bourbon, the third eligible heir to the throne. Henry Bourbon welcomed him as a refugee seeking sanctuary. However, Henry III was not as safe as he assumed. A fanatical Dominican friar, using forged papers, secretly entered the Protestant camp and murdered Henry III. The murder of Henry III left only one Henry as the rightful heir. Henry Bourbon therefore took the name of Henry IV. However, the King Philip II of Spain and the pope refused to recognize the Protestant Henry IV as king. After four years of conflict, Henry IV recognized that in order to serve as the French king, one must be a Catholic. Therefore, he converted to Catholicism. During his royal reign, however, Henry IV was benevolent to Protestants. On April 13, 1598, he issued the Edict of Nantes, granting Protestants freedom of worship, except in the city of Paris. He also he granted them legal possession of their walled cities. A peaceful and prosperous reign followed, until 1610, when a Catholic fanatic took Henry IV's life.

His son, Louis XIII, succeeded him to the throne. After 1624, Louis XIII, very active in administering his kingdom, looked to Cardinal Armand Jean du Plessis de Richelieu, the king's chief minister, to direct the affairs of state. Throughout Louis XIII reign, France developed a more centralized form of government. Although seeking to force the Huguenots to be more dependent on the king, he supported the Protestant cause during the Thirty Years' War.

The Huguenots' Influence Spreads

Calvin had his greatest influence over the French Huguenots. When Calvin lived in Geneva, French pastors traveled there in order to receive their theological training. Returning home, they worked with missionary vigor. In 1555, the Huguenots established their first congregation in Paris. Four years later, there were seventy-two Huguenot congregations. In 1559, they convened their first General Synod meeting in Paris. At that meeting, they adopted the French Confession, and approved a representative form of government. As the French Confession is a succinct summary of Calvin's theology, included below is a shortened adaptation of the confession:

> We believe and confess only one God,
> one indivisible essence,
> spiritual, eternal,
> invisible, immutable, infinite,
> incomprehensible, and ineffable.
>
> God, who can do all things,
> is all-wise, all-good,
> all just, and all-merciful.
>
> We believe that everything required for our salvation
> has been offered and communicated to us in Jesus Christ,
> the wisdom of God and God's eternal Son.
>
> Jesus Christ clothed himself in our flesh:
> God and human in one person.
>
> Through the unique sacrifice
> offered by the Lord Jesus Christ on the cross,
> we are reconciled to God—
> God's sole intention was to accomplish all righteousness
> and secure eternal life for us.
>
> We believe that we are illuminated in faith
> by the unfathomable grace of the Holy Spirit.
>
> God imparts this gracious gift.

By faith we receive grace
to live holy lives in awe and reverence for God,
for we receive what the gospel promises
when God gives us the Holy Spirit.

Faith does not cool our desire for good and holy living,
but rather engenders and excites it in us,
leading naturally to good works.

We believe that the sacraments are joined to the Word
in order that the Word may be more fully confirmed.

The sacraments are pledges to us and seals of God's grace,
giving needed aid and comfort to our faith.

Baptism is given to us as the pledge of our adoption.

In Baptism we are grafted into the body of Christ,
and renewed in holiness of life by his Spirit.

Although we are baptized only once,
the benefit it signifies lasts through life and death.

The holy Supper of our Lord is a testimony of our unity with Jesus Christ,
who died only once and was raised for our sake.

The body and blood of Jesus Christ are food and drink for the soul
just as bread and wine are nourishment for the body.

We believe that God truly and effectively gives us
what is represented in the Lord's Supper and in Baptism,
that the signs are united with the true possession
and benefit of all they present.

As for the true Church
we believe that it ought to be governed
in accordance with the order established by our Lord Jesus Christ.
No one should withdraw from the church,
satisfied to be solitary.

In this way, pure doctrine can be maintained,
the poor and afflicted can be helped in their need,
assemblies can be gathered in the name of God,
and both great and small can be edified.[1]

---

1. Presbyterian Mission Agency, "French Confession of 1559."

At one point in time, especially in the southern and western regions, French Huguenots composed 10–20 percent of the population. Following the issuing of the Edict of Nantes in 1598, the Huguenots developed into a highly literate, well-organized, and focused national religious community. Across Europe, wherever they scattered, they excelled and gained recognition as major contributors to their communities. Their experiences of suffering shaped their own emphases in Calvinism. Instead of emphasizing the moral self-examination characterized by the English Puritans, they saw their sufferings as evidence of God's election. Under Henry III and Henry IV, they experienced general toleration, although there were outbreaks of persecution. With Louis XIV's revoking of the Edict of Nantes, the resulting period of instability throughout France failed to destroy the Huguenot movement. At the same time, Catholics would develop an attitude of arrogance and exclusivity against the Huguenots. This social and religious division between the Huguenots and Catholics foreshadowed the French Revolution of 1789.

7

The Catholic Reformation

By 1560, the Protestant Reformation was sweeping over the world. Embroiled with Protestant religious fervor were Sweden, Denmark, Scotland, England, France, the Netherlands, and Germany. Only Bavaria, Portugal, Spain, and Italy remained solidly within the Catholic fold. Yet, sixty years later, the situation looked quite different. Beginning with the ascension of Pope Paul III (1534–1549), the religious tide began to shift. In France, the Huguenots sharply declined in their influence. Southern Germany was within the Catholic fold. The Catholic cause advanced on Protestantism in Austria, Poland, and Hungary. Partially, this transformation came as the result of military victories by papal forces. In particular, Huguenots lost the civil war and, during the 1590s, the duke of Parma was victorious in the southern Netherlands. However, military might alone did not reshape the religious face of Europe; instead, under Pope Paul III, the church made necessary reforms. Those ecclesiastical and theological moves ultimately led to the creation of Early Modern Catholicism.

The Establishment of Monasteries

The Roman Catholic Church, with its top-down leadership model, found change to be very difficult. The primary means of initiating change came through the creation of monastic communities, such as the Dominicans and Franciscans. In the early fifteenth century, the church created the Italian "Oratory of Divine Love," founded in Genoa in 1497, and based on the teachings of St. Catherine of Genoa (1457–1510). It stressed the celebration of the sacraments, group prayer, and care of the poor. An offshoot of the Oratory of Divine Love occurred in 1524 with the formation of the Theatines. It was an order composed of clergy, whose purpose was the reformation of the ministry of the parish clergy. In addition, 1528 saw the founding of the Capuchins, striving to be a reformed Franciscan order. Pope Paul recognized them as an order in 1536. Likewise, in 1535 the pope recognized the Ursulines as an order for women committed to virginity and charity.

Perhaps the best known of the orders founded during the sixteenth century was the Society of Jesus. Its creative leader, Ignatius Loyola (1491–1556), had served in the military until he broke his leg during the 1521 siege of Pamplona. Taken to the Montserrat Monastery, his poorly set leg was broken again and reset properly. As was typical of young men of his era, he sought out romantic novels to read. He could not find any of the scandalous reading materials in the monastery; instead, he found only devotional books, usually written by women. Bored, he began reading them, and found that the writings spoke to where he was in his own faith journey. After recuperating, he spent a year at the Manresa Monastery just outside of Barcelona. While there, he experienced visions that led to the development of his Spiritual Exercises, a program of prayer and meditation. After completing a pilgrimage to Jerusalem, Loyola studied theology, and he eventually landed at the College of Montagu of the University of Paris. Six men gathered about Loyola, all pledging to follow his Spiritual Exercises, and to take vows of chastity and poverty. Ordained as priests, in 1540, they traveled to Rome to petition the pope to recognize them as an order. Even though there was considerable opposition, Pope Paul III consented to their request, and agreed to the establishment of the Society of Jesus. This order was to be very different from the other established orders of that time. All members of the Jesuit order were highly educated clergy. In addition to the vows of poverty, chastity, and obedience, the members of the Society of Jesus further took vows to go whenever and wherever the pope might send them. Due to their special relationship with the pope, they were not accountable to the jurisdiction of regional bishops. As they must be free to travel throughout the world, they were exempt from the need to keep a periodic schedule of worship, as did the other religious houses. Instead, they committed themselves to regular spiritual retreats. Throughout the sixteenth century, the Jesuits focused their work in education, missions, and the political arena. In their missionary work, they engaged in evangelistic outreach in China and Japan, and by the seventeenth century they conducted work in the Americas. Understanding that the message of the gospel was not limited to one culture, they adopted certain local customs in order to integrate into the culture. For example, Jesuit missionaries in China were not hesitant to wear the clothing of a Confucian sage in sharing the gospel or to permit the burning of incense to honor one's ancestors. In their missionary work, they frequently used Western technology to establish positive connections with the powerful ruling classes. The more traditional Franciscan Order, disturbed over the unconventional Jesuits, petitioned the pope for relief of their grievances. In the Chinese Rites Controversy, the pope concurred with the concerns of the Franciscans, and prohibited the Jesuits from their extreme accommodations to local customs. The Jesuits likewise manifested extreme behavior in their being implicated in several assassination attempts against political leaders.

The Failure to find Common Ground Leads to the Council of Trent

At the same time, the pope made efforts to resolve the gulf between moderate Protestants and Roman Catholics. Of several meetings held, the most important one was the 1541 Regensburg Colloquy. Moderate Protestants such as Melanchthon, Calvin, Eck, and the humanist Contarini all attended. At the meeting, although they made significant progress in finding common ground, the theological gap was too wide to bridge.

The following year, perhaps due to the failure to be able to bridge the differences between Catholics and Protestants at the Regensburg Colloquy, Pope Paul III instituted the Roman Inquisition, whose purpose was to root out heresy among Catholicism. This inquisition led to torture and assassinations of dissident Catholic spokespersons. Perhaps the most well known of the inquisitions was the Spanish Inquisition. The Spanish government used the excuse of a religious inquisition as a means of ethnic cleansing, targeting influential Jewish and Muslim leaders. Paul III's successor, Pope Paul IV, continued the inquisition policies. In realizing the power of the press to shape ideas, Pope Paul IV instituted the first Index of Prohibited Books in an effort at censorship. Due to inquiring minds, however, being listed on the Index often led to a book's instant success.

Many in the Catholic Church voiced their desires for a council to address the urgent need for reform. However, powerful political and ecclesiastical voices prevented it. The Holy Roman Emperor, Charles V, called for a council to address his concerns over the political schism within Germany

The Catholic Reformation

between Lutherans and Catholics. His French political rival, Francis I, opposed his idea. Moreover, the popes were concerned that a council might revive the Conciliar Movement, and such a move might mean a reduction of their power. In the end, however, Paul IV called the Council of Trent in 1542. The Council of Trent began its deliberations in 1545. Soon, due to a power play, the council moved its deliberations to Bologna, then back to Trent. In December 1563, finally completing its work, the Council of Trent clearly defined Catholic doctrine. The Council of Trent recognized the following: Scripture and tradition were equally the source of truth; the doctrine of justification left room for works along with grace; and the seven sacraments were essential. There also were major institutional reforms at the Council of Trent, including: priests were required to live in their diocese and to be pastors to their flocks; regional theological seminaries were formed; and the Society of Jesus was formally approved. Further, they provided a standard liturgy for Mass, reaffirmed the doctrine of transubstantiation, offered only the bread to the laity, reinstated the use of the Rosary, created the "Congregation of the Holy" office to root out heresy, and reestablished the categorization of "forbidden books." In addition, at the council, the bishops increased the authority of the pope, and they added the development of a papal bureaucracy. Further, the bishops granted the bishop of Rome superior authority as the successor to Peter. All bishops from that point onward, therefore, would derive their authority from the pope, rather than directly from Christ himself. Further still, the bishops granted the pope the authority solely to interpret the actions of the council. The polity, administrative, and theological changes established by the Council of Trent lasted until the meeting of Vatican II in 1963. Nevertheless, the church was slow to change, and still struggles to implement the changes brought about by Vatican II.

9

The Legacy of the Protestant Reformers Today

Heirs of the Reformation

Early Dialogue between Catholic and Protestant Reformers

For a century and a half, the Protestant Reformation swept across Europe, interwoven with the changing social, political, and economic forces. The struggle between national religious conformity and the people's faith yearnings too frequently resulted in persecution and martyrdom. As believers, both Protestants and Catholics, we all owe a debt of gratitude to those men and women who continued to ask the vital questions of life, and to seek God's leading through their understanding of the Scriptures.

However much the Reformers might have differed theologically from the humanist scholars who chose to remain within the fold of the Catholic Church—scholars such as Desiderius Erasmus, Jacques d'Etaples, John Colet, and Thomas More—the Reformers appreciated their scholarly perceptions and achievements. For example, Erasmus' Greek New Testament greatly enhanced the biblical studies of Zwingli, Luther, and Melanchthon. However, in the face of rapidly changing social, political, and economic challenges, the Roman Catholic Church's bureaucracy insisted on institutional conformity and attempted to suppress any deviance from the officially approved norm. In their heavy-handed responses to differences from the official positions, the church's leadership transformed academic dialogue into respectful dissent, respectful dissent into open defiance, and finally, open defiance into disengagement from the mother church.

The Legacy of the Protestant Reformers Today

The Transformation in the Role of the Clergy

Among the changes, the Protestant Reformation transformed the ways in which the community members viewed the clergy. Reformation leaders rejected the idea that the clergy were to be a special caste apart from the laity. Instead, Reformation leaders insisted that the clergymen differed from the people they served only in their particular functions of ministry. In symbolizing the clergy's new role, the black Genevan gown worn in worship was not a liturgical garment. Rather, it was an academic gown—the same gown worn by law school graduates. It signified that the Reformed minister was an educated person who served God as a teacher of the Christian faith. In the Reformed church's preparation for ministry, the Reformers established challenging academic educational requirements. Frequently, these advanced educational standards also meant that the pastors were the most educated persons within their communities.

Particularly in the Church of Scotland, the symbols used within the ordination service further symbolized the transformation of the role of the minister. In the Roman Catholic ordination service, the bishop gave the newly ordained priest the keys to the church and to the font cover, a missal by which to conduct the Eucharist, a chalice to hold the sacramental wine, and vestments to wear during the celebration. In contrast, in the Reformed church's ordination service, the presbytery gave the minister a Bible from which he was to study and preach, and keys to unlock the pulpit.

In addition, in the Roman Catholic worship service, worship was a highly sensual experience. The worshipper experienced the spiritual realm through the means of paintings, hangings, statues, stained glass, elaborately painted altars, candles, the smell of incense, and music played on pipe organs. In contrast, the Protestant worship service focused on the use of the mind for the glory of God. As a result, the Reformers stripped the sanctuaries of art and transformed them into auditoriums with white-washed walls, an elevated pulpit with a sounding board for voice projection, a baptismal font, a simple Communion table, and a liturgy focusing on the reading of the Scriptures and the preaching of lengthy biblical expository sermons. Only in the Netherlands did the Reformed churches continue to retain the elaborate pipe organs. In addition, on Sundays there was a prolonged ringing of the church bells in calling the faithful to worship. As the people filtered into the sanctuary, an elder read aloud from the scriptures. At the appointed hour of worship, the elders locked the church doors for the remainder of the service. In some places, congregations participated in the preaching event by shouting loudly "Amen" or other approving faith expressions. On arriving home following the service, parents quizzed their children and servants on the content of the morning sermon.

The Role of the Church and Poverty

In medieval Catholic cultures, the church taught that poverty was a virtue: as one suffered poverty in this life, so they might achieve a rich heavenly reward in the life to come. The church further promoted institutional poverty in the form of the begging and mendicant friars, and sought to relieve the suffering of the poor and disenfranchised through acts of individual charity and compassion.

Concurrently, Catholic and Reformed Christian humanists emphasized the vital personal relationships that people have within their own communities. In accord, Calvinistic reformers likewise stressed that God's salvation was not limited to God's saving of individual souls. Moreover, God's salvation extended to the human transformation of society for the betterment of all persons—there was a public responsibility for helping the poor and disenfranchised. Beginning with Martin Luther, many Protestant towns banned begging as an occupation and required public financial support of projects to help the needy, including providing temporary workhouses for the poor.

The Reformation and the Role of Women

The Protestant Reformation brought about a mixed bag for women. The Catholic Church understood sexual abstinence as a divine gift, after the model of the Virgin Mary. Yet, it encouraged houses of prostitution as a means of relieving the sexual tension of young men. In contrast to the Catholic model, the Protestant communities closed their houses of prostitution, and promoted marriage as the proper place for sexual gratification. Further, the Reformers—Luther, Melanchthon, Zwingli, and Calvin—all stressed the ordinance of marriage and the importance of the family life. In part, Luther purposely wrote his Small Catechism to give guidance to parents in the Christian education of their children.

Given the historic physical vulnerability of women, the legal ability for women to divorce their husbands has been an important basic human rights protection. In the Roman Catholic Church, Augustine referred to marriage as a sacrament, thereby prohibiting divorce. In the thirteenth century, Thomas Aquinas approved of Augustine's teachings on the indissolubility of marriage. At the Council of Trent, in 1563, the Roman Catholic Church placed into cannon law the indissolubility of a consummated Christian marriage. At the same time, the Catholic Church approved long-term separation as an option to divorce, as well as continued the practice of the annulment of marriages. In contrast to the position of the Roman Catholic Church, Luther accepted divorce as a necessary option in cases of adultery, impotence, refusal of conjugal rights, and desertion. Melanchthon, Luther's colleague, however, limited divorce to infidelity and desertion. John Calvin and Theodore Beza allowed divorce for adultery, desertion, and whenever there were irreconcilable religious differences. In 1561, Geneva took the liberal stance of permitting divorce on the grounds of adultery and irreconcilable religious differences. Zwingli and Bucer took a more permissive stance, adding as permissive grounds: abandonment, endangerment of life, and insanity.

Martin Luther persuaded Frederick III to close the monasteries and convents. However, in closing the convents, he restricted many of the professional vocational opportunities available for women. This was due to the fact that, as members of the Roman Catholic orders, women were administrators of significantly large church institutions, and provided significant social services to persons in need. In a strange paradox of thought, although Luther was not prepared to promote women to church leadership positions, he appreciated the intellectual abilities of women. In 1520, he proposed that women learn to read the Bible in German or Latin. Later, he broadened his proposal, to use the funds approved for the benefit of begging friars instead be used for the establishment of schools, staffed by women, for the education of girls and young women. Additionally, Luther once even compared women's ability to learn very favorably with the so-called learned men of the corrupt Roman Catholic establishment. Certainly, Luther's wife, Kate, as well as the wives of the other Reformers, greatly influenced their husbands' thinking. Kate managed a household that consisted of up to thirty to forty persons, including children, servants, as well as boarders staying with the family. Later in her life, she managed a farm that Luther received as a gift. As a further indication of the influence of women over the Reformation movement, of those burned at the stake by Mary Tudor, a high percentage were women (51 percent out of about 280 persons). Later, the Protestant Queen Elizabeth I amazed foreign ambassadors with her fluent Latin and her understanding of the political arena. Although the Reformation did not bring about many opportunities for women, it did overall improve their general lot in life.

The Attacks on Witchcraft

During the late fifteenth century until the close of the eighteenth century, large-scale persecutions of witches took place. The courts tried some 100,000 persons (mostly women) for witchcraft, with perhaps about 40,000 persons burned at the stake. The most extensive periods of persecution occurred within twenty to thirty years either side of 1600. These witchcraft persecutions took place during the same period as the most violent Catholic-Protestant conflicts. The people in the villages tolerated such social deviates in the past. However, due to the emerging desire for conformity, Catholics and Protestants began to look upon these older eccentric women with suspicion. With the apocalyptic emphasis of the time, people began to associate such deviates as manifestations of the devil. The worst persecutors of witches were the Catholic prince-bishops in the small German territories. Fortunately for women, in Calvin's Geneva they burned few witches, and there almost were no trials in the Netherlands or Calvinist Palatinate. However, in other Protestant areas, particularly Scotland, such persecutions were intense and continued into the 1660s. The Calvinist Puritan colony of Massachusetts experienced the famous Salem witch trials of 1692.

Advancements in the Liberal Arts and Sciences

The Reformation leaders and the humanist leaders sought to develop creative means of education. With exceptions, while the humanist leadership focused their efforts on developing universities, the Reformation leadership focused their efforts on developing primary and secondary schools. With their emphasis on people understanding the Scriptures, the Protestant leaders wanted the masses to be able to read the Scriptures themselves.

In May 1543, Nicolaus Copernicus, a Polish cannon and astronomer, printed in Nuremberg his earth-shaking work, *On the Revolution of the Celestial Spheres*. In it, he asserted that the earth was not at the center of the universe; instead, the earth rotated around the sun. The church immediately condemned his book. Even Martin Luther questioned his assertions, although he felt that such scientific studies must continue.

Within a month, Andreas Vesalius published his book *On the Structure of the Human Body*, in which he described basic human anatomy. Ambrose Paré in 1545 published his studies in surgery, based on his experiences in the Franco-Habsburg wars of the 1540s. Many scholars later recognized him as the father of modern surgery. Later, in 1628, William Harvey advanced his theory on the blood circulatory system. The floodgates opened, and a number of additional publications appeared in the areas of arithmetic, geometry, botany, zoology, geography, and ballistics.

Concurrent with the Reformation era, the Renaissance brought about new directions in the arts and sciences. In 1552, Christopher Marlow wrote *Doctor Faustus*, which dramatized the excitement and yet the dangers of scientific inquiry and speculation. In his story, Faustus sold his soul to the devil in seeking to obtain the powers over life and death. Ultimately, he was condemned to hell.

With the coming of the tenth century, increased sharing of knowledge took place between the Christian and Islamic worlds, particularly knowledge gained from the libraries in Toledo and in Baghdad. This increased sharing of knowledge eventually led to significant advances in medicine and astronomy. In the twelfth century, Gerard Cremova of Toledo translated into Latin the tenth-century Arabic scholar Avicenna's studies in the writings of Galen and Aristotle. Avicenna's studies became the standard medical textbook in European universities.

Leonardo da Vinci spanned the gap that existed between the arts and sciences. Unfortunately, da Vinci did not publish his works, and they would have been lost to posterity if not for the nineteenth-century writer Walter Pater.

Although Plato and Aristotle exerted considerable influence over the arts and sciences during the sixteenth century, as the century closed their influence waned. The discovery of America led many to realize that a new era was breaking in upon them, and these ancient sources were limited in the knowledge that they could impart. For example, in the early seventeenth century, Galileo disapproved of Aristotle's theories of motion, acceleration, and the nature of the universe. Sir Francis Bacon likewise rejected Aristotle's teachings and argued for empirical observation of scientific analysis. In the emerging European scientific community, modern scientific methods were coming of age and were replacing the wisdoms of the ancient teachers. Yet, for all the advancements that the scientific age brought to humanity, there was an inherent danger; for a break with the moral compass of philosophy and the Judeo-Christian faith tradition left science devoid of an ethical center. The results of an unrestrained science bought about the horrors of modern warfare.

The Importance of the Scriptures as the Compass for Decision Making

The most important contribution of the Reformation was its emphasis on the Holy Spirit speaking through the Scriptures as the defining compass for Christian ethics. In the Catholic Church, the celebration of the Lord's Supper was the central element of worship. The elevated altar, with a communion rail separating the chancel from the nave, was the focus of the sanctuary. The Catholic Church honored the Scriptures by kissing the Bible and carrying it into the liturgical procession. Yet the priests seldom read or preached sermons based on the Scriptures. Moreover, as the worship service was in Latin, a foreign tongue, the people could not understand any of the words when the priest read the Scriptures or celebrated the Eucharist. The people simply felt God's redeeming grace conveyed to them through the eucharistic sacrifice. In contrast, the Reformers understood the reading and the hearing of the Scriptures as the central focus of worship. In accord with their theology, they altered the sanctuaries to have an elevated pulpit, a baptismal font, and a Communion table in the midst of the people. These architectural elements physically demonstrated the unity of the written and preached Word of God, the engrafting of the people into Christ through the waters of baptism, and the spiritually sustaining celebration of the Lord's Supper. Although John Calvin desired for the celebration of weekly Communion, the Geneva city council authorized only quarterly Communion. Of course, the approved quarterly celebration was an increase over the previous Catholic tradition of an annual celebration. John Calvin likewise understood the importance of music for conveying the faith. He insisted that the musical texts should be in the language of the people. Second, there should only be one note per syllable, such as in the familiar setting of "Old Hundredth," "All-people-that-on-earth-do dwell." In encouraging singing of the Psalms, Calvin and Bucer compiled the *Genevan Psalter*. Translated into French, and set to music, he published it in a nondescript pocketsize volume that one could hide in clothing. The *Genevan Psalter* became very instrumental in the French Huguenot movement.

The Reformed Church Lives between the Past and the Future

The Reformation period occurred centuries ago, and it expressed itself in a very different worldview from that of today. Although it was an important element of the emergence of Early Modern Europe, culturally it was closer to the medieval period than to our twenty-first-century world. When Martin Luther was born, Columbus had not yet sailed from Spain in search of a new passage to India. When Martin Luther took orders to become a monk, the Jamestown settlement in Virginia was yet a century away. When Martin Luther appeared before the Diet of Worms and declared that his "conscience was captive to the Word of God," it would be yet another 110 years before the English Puritans would begin journeying to America. The fifteenth and sixteenth centuries were an era in which there were no paved interstate highways, no harnessing of electricity, no centrally heated and air-conditioned buildings, no television or 24/7 news channels, no gasoline engines, and quick means of transportation by air, sea, or land. It was an era in which there were no telephones, texting, computers, email, faxing, ballpoint pens, or legal pads. Further, there was no understanding of the environmental effects of pollution, the expansion of the universe, use of robots, lasers, and antibiotics in medicine, or the manipulation of genes. The medieval church taught that the earth was the center of the universe; hand-drawn world maps centered on Jerusalem, and even in their wildest imaginations people could not have envisioned satellites spinning about earth, or spacecraft exploring the planet Mars.

Yet, as we do, these ancestors in the faith sought to understand God's activity in the world. Although five hundred years of earth-shaking changes separate us, their witness to God's sustaining and liberating power in the world continues as a testimony to us as we too seek to be faithful disciples in our own time. Therefore, instead of mimicking their testimony, we must be able and willing to continue the faith conversations that they began long ago.

The Protestant Reformation Was Providential

In his book *Theology for Liberal Protestants*, Douglas Ottati helps to identify how the Protestant Reformation was formed, and what can be learned from those formational dynamics. He writes about the "emergence" scenario proposed by the biochemist Pier Luigi Luisi regarding how life began:

[molecular complexity is] . . . "accomplished by the onset of novel properties—up to the point where self-reproduction and eventually life itself arises." To describe this process, Luisi makes use of the philosophical idea of *emergence*, which, he says, refers to the advent of novel properties that cannot be described in terms of initial constituents. An example is the formation of water from its atomic components, "The collective properties of water are not present in hydrogen and oxygen, so the properties of water can be viewed as emergent ones." That is, while the atomic structure of water consists of the basic components of hydrogen and oxygen, the properties of water cannot be reduced to the properties of hydrogen and oxygen. A new relatedness of parts gives rise to properties that cannot be deduced to the properties of the components . . .[1]

. . . The formation of a human community or culture may also be viewed as the emergence of an ensemble with properties or characteristics that were not previously present. Here as in the story of the beginning of the people of Israel, individuals, families, and tribes (or similar ensembles) combine to constitute a more complex social entity. Their coming together depends on historic vitalities and occurrences that fashion the original core of the community but are controlled by no single individual or tribe. Indeed, Israel, the historic entity that results and perdures over generations through peril and promise, turns out to be something more and something other than any of its original leaders and architects intended or expected. . . There are contingencies that we cannot eliminate.[2]

Ottati further writes, "Ensembles (stars, planetary systems, ecologies, organisms, communities, and so on) continue. A third dynamic is that over time, ensembles destabilize and dissipate, critical relationships, processes, and patterns deteriorate, alter, and cease."[3]

Likewise, the Protestant Reformation did not occur in an environmental, socioeconomic vacuum. Instead, a number of forces and factors came together in a particular time and place, giving birth to the emergence of the Protestant Reformation movement. It is important to realize that, although the Protestant Reformation movement developed as the result of visionary thinkers, it developed in ways unforeseen by the original

1. Ottati, *Theology for Liberal Protestants*, 347.
2. Ibid., 348.
3. Ibid., 349.

proponents. For example, Martin Luther in nailing his Ninety-Five Theses on the church door at Wittenberg was seeking a scholarly debate within the Roman Catholic Church. Yet, his naivety and temperament placed him in peril of execution. Nevertheless, protectors such as Holy Roman Emperor Charles V allowed him safe passage from the Diet of Worms, and Elector Frederick provided him sanctuary at Wartburg Castle, thereby enabling the Reformation movement to continue. In addition, the lack of a centralized German governmental authority enabled multiple printing presses within the country to produce Luther's controversial writings, unlike Catholic England, with its centralized governmental control of the printing presses. In addition, the competing international situation, the decrease in the ravaging effects of the Black Death, and the development of an emerging middle class all contributed to the formation of the Protestant Reformation. Moreover, John Calvin's narrow escape from a Paris upstairs bedroom, his stopping at a Geneva inn for the night, his encounter with Farel, his writing of his "Reply to Sadolet," Bucer's invitation to Strasbourg, and his return to Geneva—in all of these separate and isolated seeming events, in hindsight, God's providential handiwork is evident.

The Church Needs a New Reformation

Throughout the Reformation era, the Roman Catholic Church failed adequately to adapt to the needs of the changing environment of Early Modern Europe. Yet, in God's grace, after centuries of the church locking itself into past eras, Pope John XXIII called the Second Vatican Council into session (1962–1965). The Roman Catholic Church took a quantum leap in ministry. As a result, priests celebrated the Mass in the language of the local congregations, worship included a public confession of sins and new hymns, fasting practices revised, preaching was given greater emphasis, and priests gave both the bread and the wine during Eucharist. At the same time, biblical and theological studies increased. Vatican II continues to have repercussions within the Roman Catholic Church. The decisions that the Catholic bishops made at Vatican II likewise have continued influencing Protestants, to include the adoption of a new common lectionary based on the lectionary developed by Vatican II, use of the alb and other colorful vestments and hangings during worship, more frequent celebration of the Eucharist, and a greater appreciation of our common church history. We can celebrate the many of the goals of the original Protestant Reformers are a reality. Concurrently, however, since the 1960s, Protestant congregations have experienced a changing environment, along with declining and aging membership, as well as theological schisms that rock the unity of the Holy Catholic Church. Some church leaders attempt to meet that crisis through the creation of shallow worship experiences that evoke a "feeling good about oneself" mentality, louder and louder bands that drown out the voices of worshipping congregations, or preaching that mimics after-dinner motivational speeches. Yet, these attempts to bolster church attendance betray our historic identity as Reformed Protestants. Instead, we need to reclaim our identity as Reformed Protestants in meeting the challenges of a new age. Firstly, we need to identify our heritage in Reformed Protestantism; secondly, we need to identify what God is calling us to be as Reformed Protestants in the twenty-first century; and thirdly, we need to identify the mission field that God is laying before us for witness and service. In gaining a sense of our identity as Reformed Protestants, we need to return to the basics, developing creative managers and visionary leaders for our congregations and councils, as well as emphasizing biblically based preaching and teaching in our congregations.

John P. Kotter writes of the need for creative managers for the purpose of:

> . . . establishing steps and timetables for achieving needed results, then allocating the resources necessary to make it happen . . . establishing some structures for accomplishing plan requirements, staffing that structure with individuals, delegating responsibility and authority for carrying out the plan, proposing policies and procedures to help guide people, and creating methods or systems to monitor implementation. . . . monitoring results, identifying deviations from the plan, then planning and organizing to solve these problems . . . producing a degree of predictability and order and has the potential to constantly produce the short-term results expected by various stakeholders . . .

He likewise writes regarding the need for visionary leaders for:

> establishing direction: developing a vision of the future—often the distant future—and strategies for producing the changes needed to achieve that vision . . . communicating direction in words and deeds to all those whose cooperation may be needed so as to influence the creation of teams and coalitions to understand the vision and the strategies and that accept their validity . . . energizing people to overcome major political, bureaucratic, and resource

barriers to change by satisfying basic, but often unfilled, human needs . . . produce change, often to a dramatic degree, and has the potential to produce extremely useful change . . .[4]

Yet, without managers, leaders' vision fails to implement the adapted changes needed; and without the visionary leaders, the system begins to stagnate. Within congregations, there are laity and church officers that are highly skilled at managing as well as providing visionary leadership for secular institutions. The church leadership therefore needs to bring forth the gifts inherent within the congregational leadership and to provide for continuing skill development.

Moreover, Kotter writes about the leadership styles essential for an organization to meet the environmental challenges:

> Management is a set of processes that can keep a complicated system of people and technology running smoothly. The most important aspects of management include planning, budgeting, organizing, staffing, controlling, and problem solving. Leadership is a set of processes that creates organizations in the first place or adapts them to significantly changing circumstances. Leadership defines what the future should look like, aligns people to that vision, and inspires them to make it happen despite the obstacles.[5]

In addition to developing church leaders, the church needs to reclaim the reformers' emphasis on biblically based teaching and preaching. That is, in preaching and teaching, helping congregations to understand the particular Scripture's original context, and allowing the Holy Spirit to transform God's written Word into God's revealed Living Word for today's church. Given the laity's sad lack of biblical knowledge and skills in historical-critical biblical interpretation, the church needs to reclaim the "neo-orthodox" emphasis on teaching and preaching. Of course, the setting for preaching and teaching might vary. In an effort to reach the "unchurched" and "non-believers," congregations might rent rooms in neutral public areas such as shopping malls or movie theaters, or purchasing weekday time on talk radio stations for short homilies. Of course, biblically based teaching and preaching cannot exclude the other pastoral and congregational leadership functions. Yet, too often, pastors and governing bodies have allowed non-urgent pastoral concerns within the congregation, and trivial administrative functions, to intrude upon the needed preparation time for

---

4. Kotter, *Leading Change*, 26.
5. Ibid., 25.

the ministers' teaching and preaching ministries. During the early to mid-twentieth century, the pastor's study was the place for reading, prayer, as well as sermon and teaching preparation. Sadly, the "study" has been transformed into the pastor's "office," where the pastor oversees the details of the church's day-to-day operations. As a part of this shift in ministerial roles, we have lost the primary role of the pastor—that of teaching and preaching. The result is that in many congregations, the membership lacks the basic knowledge of how to apply Reformed biblical and theological thinking to ecclesiastical and secular decisions. Congregational leadership is challenging. It requires that clergypersons manage their time to give significant priority to the preaching and teaching ministry. The Reformers were biblically based preachers and teachers who enabled their congregations to catch the vision of the glory of God, and God's calling to serve as God's hands in the world. Likewise, today, in partnership with other professionally trained church educators, clergypersons are to train and empower the laity to fulfill their ministry in the world. In January 1964, the singer-songwriter Bob Dylan released his song, "The Times They Are a-Changin'." The first stanza is as follows:

> Come gather 'round people
> Wherever you roam
> And admit that the waters
> Around you have grown
> And accept that soon
> You'll be drenched to the bone
> If your time to you is worth savin'
> Then you better start swimmin' or you'll sink like a stone
> For the times they are a-changin' . . .[6]

In his song, Bob Dylan was verbalizing the massive social, religious, economic, and political tsunami that was sweeping throughout the world in the early 1960s. Those turbulent surging waters of change transformed the social, religious, economic, and political landscape, and they continue to shape the ways that we think and act to the present time. The question for the church is whether it will attempt to deny the changes that still are taking place around us, or whether the church, Protestant and Catholic, will creatively use the power generated in the massive cultural wave for the glory of God.

6. Taken from http://www.bobdylan.com/us/songs/times-they-are-changin.

Appendix A

The Reformation Confessions

The Schleitheim Confession

The Anabaptist movement rejected infant baptism due to their interpretations of Scripture. Oppressed for their beliefs, an element of the Anabaptist movement, the Swiss Brethren, scattered throughout southern Germany. In 1527, the leadership met in the city of Schleitheim and formulated the Schleitheim Confession. Through it, the Swiss Brethren established boundaries for restraint within their own fellowship, as well as drew a line between their beliefs and the Zwinglian reformers. Most Anabaptist groups eventually adopted the confession as their own statement of faith.

The Augsburg Confession

First read to the Diet of Augsburg on June 25, 1530, the Augsburg Confession is one of the finest positive expressions of Martin Luther's theology. Although Luther had a major hand in the initial composition of the document, Philip Melanchthon was the final editor. Most of the Augsburg Confession drew upon Luther's preceding works, especially the Torgau Articles, which Luther directed toward abuses in the Roman Catholic Church, and the Schwabach Articles for their sound doctrinal statements. Even though some of the Protestant princes disagreed on points in the confession, they approved it as a united front against the aggression of the Catholic Holy Roman Emperor Charles V.

The Scots Confession

John Knox, the Scottish reformer and student of John Calvin, wrote the Scots Confession in 1560. The Church of Scotland ratified it on August 17, 1560, and it remained the official faith statement until 1688, when the Church of Scotland adopted the Westminster Confession. It is a refreshing confession, defining the critical theological stances of the Reformed faith. Particularly significant is its definition of the true church as existing wherever there is "the true preaching of the Word of God . . . the right administrations of the sacraments of Christ Jesus . . . (and) ecclesiastical discipline uprightly ministered . . ." It further subordinates all to the rule and lordship of Jesus Christ as the Head of the Church.

The Belgic Confession

Throughout the Netherlands, many people identified the Protestant struggle with the political struggle for national autonomy against the encroachments of the Catholic Spanish King Phillip II. In 1562, the Calvinistic leaders formulated the Belgic Confession in expressing their faith. Closely modeled after the 1559 French (or Gallic) Confession, the Belgic Confession differs in its expression of the more radical Calvinism of the Netherlands, an expanded discussion of the doctrine of the Trinity, and the difference between Calvinism and the Anabaptist movement.

The Heidelberg Catechism

In 1563, Zacharias Ursinus and Casper Olevianus formulated the Heidelberg Catechism. The catechism, written at the request of the ruler of the Palatinate, was an effort to resolve the conflicts between the Calvinists and the Lutherans. Expressed in the second person, it brings together the doctrines of repentance, faith, and love. It further includes statements on the meaning of the Apostles' Creed, the Lord's Prayer, the Ten Commandments, and the sacraments. Divided into fifty-two sections so that congregations might use it on Sundays, it is fresh and lively in its style, and offers a dignified, brief, and eloquent confession of faith. Particularly, the first question, "What is your only comfort, in life and in death?" has been meaningful for the church for centuries.

The Reformation Confessions

The Second Helvetic Confession

In 1566, Henry Bullinger, a leader in the Reformation movement, composed the Second Helvetic Confession in Zurich, Switzerland. When the Lutherans charged him with heresy, he submitted the Second Helvetic Confession as his personal statement of faith. The confession states that the Reformed faith is in harmony with the universal faith of the ages, and that Christians can disagree on matters that are not essential for salvation.

The Westminster Confession of Faith and Catechisms

From 1644 to 1649, the Puritan leaders formulated the Westminster Confession of Faith and Catechisms in London at Westminster Cathedral. Initially a political document, written on the direction of the English Parliament, it provided a mediating theological position between the Anglicans and Puritans. There were two catechisms, one written for the instruction of adults and one for the instruction of children. Although approved by Parliament, it never became an official document of the Church of England. However, it became the official confession of faith for the Church of Scotland. Chapter 3, "Of God's Eternal Decrees," was controversial in the church due to its harsh doctrine of "double predestination."

Appendix B

Brief Timeline of Reformation Era Events

563	Columba comes to Scotland, establishes church on island of Iona
732	Charles Martel stops Turks at Battle of Tours
1000	First universities chartered
1150	Margaret, wife of Scottish King Malcolm II, transforms "Old Celtic Church"
1224	Thomas Aquinas born
1274	Thomas Aquinas dies at fifty years old on way to Council of Lyons
1330	John Wycliffe born
1347	Black Death first appears in Crimea; Mainz and Cologne exterminated as well as blamed for the Bubonic Plague; 2000 Strasbourg Jews murdered
1349	Thomas Bradwardine, early Catholic reformer, dies
1378–1417	Great Schism between rival claims to papacy
1384	John Wycliffe dies
1397	Medici Bank established in Florence
1409	Council of Pisa
1414–18	Council of Constance
1415	John Huss executed; John Wycliffe condemned as heretic/body exhumed and burned

Brief Timeline of Reformation Era Events

1440	Frederick II elected as Holy Roman Emperor; Donation of Constantine proven as forgery
1450	Gutenberg invents printing press with movable type
1453	Constantinople falls to Turks; end of the Hundred-Years War
1456	Gutenberg Bible printed
1459	Gozzoli paints "Adoration of the Magi"
1466	Black Death kills 400,000 people in Paris
1466/1469	Desiderius Erasmus born
1472–1500	214 mathematical books published in Italy
1478	Spanish Inquisition begins
1482	Printing press in Germany publishes Ptolemy's *Geography*, a second-century map, updated with latitude and longitude that reshaped perceptions of the world
1483	Martin Luther born
1484	Huldrych Zwingli born
1485	Tudor dynasty begins reign in England
1488	Dias sails around the Cape of Good Hope
1492	Columbus discovers America; Spanish defeat Moors in Granada; Jews expelled from Spain; German cloth merchant Martin Behaim creates first modern terrestrial globe in Nuremberg
1497	Jews expelled from Portugal; Vasco da Gama reaches India
1498	Leonardo da Vinci completes studies for a casting pit for the casting of Sforza horse
1500	Pedro Álvarez Cabral arrives in Brazil
1505	Luther becomes an Augustinian friar at Erfurt; Leonardo paints *Mona Lisa*
1506	Donato Bramante begins working on St. Peter's in Rome
1507	Giovanni Bellinis complete the painting *St. Mark Preaching in Alexandria*

Brief Timeline of Reformation Era Events

1506	Zwingli graduates from University of Basal; ordained parish priest
1509	John Calvin born; Henry VIII becomes English king
1511	Erasmus publishes *In Praise of Folly*
1512	Michelangelo completes painting Sistine Chapel ceiling; Erasmus publishes *De Copia*.
1512	Michelangelo finishes the ceiling of the Sistine Chapel
1513	Niccolò Machiavelli writes *The Prince*
1513	Hernán Cortés arrives in Mexico; Machiavelli writes *The Prince*
1514	John Knox born
1515	Francis I ascends to the French throne
1516	Charles I becomes king of Spain; Erasmus finishes his Greek New Testament; Thomas More writes *Utopia*
1517	Luther posts his Ninety-Five Theses
1519	Luther debates Johan Eck in Leipzig; Charles V becomes Holy Roman Emperor
1520–21	Luther excommunicated—burns papal bull; Ferdinand Magellan reaches the Pacific; Sultan Suleiman ascends to throne of Ottoman Empire, opening up artistic and diplomatic exchanges between East and West
1521	Luther at Diet of Worms—goes into hiding
1522	Luther translates the New Testament; Zwingli violates Lent by eating sausage in Zurich; Zwingli secretly marries
1523	Two Augustinian monks burned at stake in Rome; Zwingli begins Reformation in Zurich; Calvin enters University of Paris to study for priesthood
1524	Luther and Johan Walter produce first Protestant hymnal; Zwingli's marriage becomes public knowledge; Raphael completes propaganda painting of the Donation of Constantine for the Vatican in order to show shift in power from East to West
1524–25	Peasants' War in Germany

Brief Timeline of Reformation Era Events

1525	Luther marries Katherine von Bora; Erasmus breaks with Luther over *Freedom of the Will*
1527	Zurich reformation leaders burn at stake first Anabaptists
1529	Protest at Diet of Speyer gives name to Protestants; Failure of Luther and Zwingli to agree on meaning of Lord's Supper; Switzerland engages in first of religious wars
1530	Lutheran Augsburg Confession approved by Diet of Augsburg
1531	Lutheran League at Schmalkaldic fights against Charles V; Zwingli killed in Second Swiss War; Calvin's father dies and Calvin enters Orleans to pursue study of the law
1533	Henry VIII breaks with Rome; Hans Holbein completes painting *The Ambassadors*, an icon of the Renaissance
1534	Francis I of France crackdowns on Protestants; Calvin flees Paris; Loyola founds Society of Jesus
1535	Bishop Thomas More executed
1536	Calvin's first edition of the *Institutes of the Christian Religion* published and his first sermon preached at St. Peter's Cathedral in Geneva
1538	Calvin leaves Geneva for Strasbourg
1540	Jesuits formally recognized by pope; Calvin marries Idelette deBure; Geneva city council asks Calvin to return to Geneva
1541	Calvin returns to Geneva
1542	Inquisition begins; Idelette deBure gives birth to baby boy, who later dies
1543	Nicolaus Copernicus publishes *On the Revelation of the Celestial Spheres*, Andreas Vesalius publishes *On the Structure of the Human Body*
1543	Portuguese sailors reach Japan; Andreas Vesalius publishes *On the Structure of the Human Body*; Luther writes pamphlet *On the Jews and their Lies*
1545	Ambrose Pare, the father of modern surgery, publishes his first book on surgery

Brief Timeline of Reformation Era Events

1545–47	First session of Council of Trent
1546–47	Schmalkaldic War
1545	On order from Cardinal Beaton, George Wishart taken prisoner at St. Andrews Castle
1546	Wishart burned at stake; Calvinists capture St. Andrews castle, execute Cardinal Beaton in revenge for Wishart's death; Catholic troops storm castle and imprison Knox as galley slave; Luther dies
1547	Henry VIII dies; Reign of Edward VI begins; Idelette deBure dies
1549	Edward VI *Book of Common Prayer*
1551–52	Second session of Council of Trent
1552	Christopher Marlow publishes *Doctor Faustus*
1552	Edward VI revise s*Book of Common Prayer*; publication of the Forty-Two Articles
1553	Michael Servetus burned at stake in Geneva; Mary I restores Catholicism in England
1555	Peace of Augsburg; Knox flees Scotland and studies for three years with Calvin
1556	Charles V abdicates as king; Philip II becomes Spanish king
1558	Mary I (Tudor) dies; Elizabeth I becomes English queen
1559	Elizabeth I issues *Book of Common Prayer*
1559	Papal index of forbidden books published; Knox returns to Scotland; Huguenots organize first General Synod in Paris
1559–60	John Knox leads Reformation in Scotland; Scots Confession completed
1560	Melanchthon dies
1562	Thirty-Nine Articles under Elizabeth I
1562–63	Third session of Council of Trent
1560	Scottish Parliament adopts Scots Confession as official doctrinal statement of Church of Scotland; first General Assembly meets; Knox's wife Marjorie dies

Brief Timeline of Reformation Era Events

1561	Mary Queen of Scots arrives in Scotland
1562	Belgic Confession completed
1563–1665	Black Death strikes London six times
1563	Frederick III establishes Calvinism in Palatinate; Heidelberg Catechism adopted
1564	John Calvin dies; William Shakespeare born; Galileo born; Knox marries Margaret Stewart
1566	Second Helvetic Confession completed
1567	Dutch revolt against Spain
1568	Mary Queen of Scots flees to England
1570	Pope Pius V excommunicates Elizabeth I
1571	Christian naval forces defeat Turks at Lepanto
1572	St. Bartholomew's Day Massacre in Paris; John Knox dies in Edinburgh
1577	Formula of Concord reunites German Lutherans
1582	Gregory XIII changes the calendar
1584	Queen Elizabeth grants Sir Walter Raleigh charter to explore new world
1588	English defeat attempted invasion by Spanish Armada
1589	Huguenot Henry III of France assassinated; Henry of Navarra installed as Henry IV
1590	Spenser writes *The Faerie Queene*
1593	Henry IV converts to Catholicism
1598	Edict of Nantes grants limited religious freedom to Huguenots in France
1603	Elizabeth I dies; James I ascends to throne, uniting Scotland and England; Shakespeare composes *Othello*
1604	Cervantes composes *Don Quixote*
1605	Gunpowder plot to blow up English Parliament—Jesuits implicated among plotters; Bacon writes *Advancement of Learning*

Brief Timeline of Reformation Era Events

1607	Jamestown Colony established in Virginia
1618	Thirty-Year War breaks out
1619	Synod of Dort and acceptance of TULIP doctrines
1622	Papal Congregation of Propaganda Fide (for missions) established
1628	William Harvey advances his theory of blood circulatory system
1629	Charles I grants royal charter to colony of Massachusetts
1633	Galileo condemned for heresy by Inquisition
1637	James I declared that Presbyterians must use the 1549 Prayer Book—Jenny Geddes starts riot in St. Giles Church
1638	National Covenant signed in Scotland
1641	Catholic rebellion in Ireland
1642	English Civil War breaks out
1648	Treaty of Westphalia ends Thirty-Year War
1649	Westminster Confession adopted by English Parliament
1649	Charles I executed; Puritan reign begins; Westminster Confession completed
1660	Charles II installed and reestablishes Anglican Church
1685	Louis IV revokes Edict of Nantes
1688–89	Glorious Revolution deposes Catholic James II
1692	Salem witch trials
1702–11	Huguenots rebel in France
1721	Black Death appears in Marseille, France

Bibliography

Atkinson, James. "Martin Bucer (1491–1551) – Ecumenical Pioneer." *Churchman* 79/1 (1965). Online: http://archive.churchsociety.org/churchman/documents/Cman_079_1_Atkinson.pdf.
Brotton, Jerry. *The Renaissance: A Very Short Introduction*. New York: Oxford University Press, 2006.
Calvin, John. *Institutes of the Christian Religion*. Translated by Ford Lewis Battles, edited by John T. McNeill. Library of Christian Classics 20. Philadelphia: Westminster, 1967.
———. *Theological Treatises*. Translated by and edited by J. K. S. Reid. Library of Christian Classics 22. Louisville: Westminster, 1954.
Caldwell, Simon. "Book Bound in Skin of Executed Jesuits Sells at Auction in England." Catholic News Service, December 3, 2007. Online: http://www.catholicnews.com/data/stories/cns/0706792.htm.
Chadwick, Henry. *Augustine*. New York: Oxford University Press, 1986.
George, Timothy, editor. *John Calvin and the Church: A Prism of Reform*. Louisville: Westminster, 1990.
Godfrey, W. Robert. *John Calvin: Pilgrim and Pastor*. Wheaton, IL: Crossway, 2009.
Gonzalez, Justo L. "How the Bible Has Been Interpreted In Christian Tradition." In *New Interpreter's Bible*, edited by Leander E. Keck, 1:83–106. Nashville: Abingdon, 1994. Online: http://fontes.lstc.edu/~rklein/Documents/gonzalez.htm.
Gonzalez, Justo L. *The Story of Christianity*. 2 vols. San Francisco: Harper and Row, 1985.
Gorman, Michael. "Divorce and Remarriage from Augustine to Zwingli." *Christianity Today*, August 31, 2000. Online: http://www.christanitytoday.com.com/ct/2000/augustweb—only/46.0c.html.
Huppert, George. *After the Black Death: A Social History of Early Modern Europe*. Bloomington: Indiana University Press, 1986.
Klug, Eugene F. "Luther's Contribution to the Augsburg Confession." *Concordia Theological Quarterly* 44/2–3 (1980) 155–72. Online: http://www.ctsfw.net/media/pdfs/klugluthersontribution.pdf.
Kotter, John P. *Leading Change*. Boston: Harvard Business School Press, 1996.
Lefler, Hugh Talmage, and Albert Ray Newsome. *North Carolina: The History of a Southern State*. Rev. ed. Chapel Hill: University of North Carolina Press, 1963.
Lingle, Walter L. *Presbyterian: Their History and Beliefs*. Revised by T. Watson Street. Louisville: John Knox, 1965.
MacCulloch, Diarmaid. *The Boy King: Edward VI and the Protestant Reformation*. New York: Palgrave, 2001.

Bibliography

———. *The Reformation: A History*. New York: Penguin, 2003.
Madrigal, Alexis C. "It Was Once 'Somewhat Common' to Bind Books With Human Skin." *The Atlantic*, April 3, 2014. Online: http://www.theatlantic.com/technology/archive/2014/04/it-was-once-somewhat-common-to-bind-books-with-human-skin/360145.
Marshall, Peter. *The Reformation: A Very Short Introduction*. New York: Oxford University Press, 2009.
McCormack, Bruce. "Christ and the Decree: An Unsettled Question for the Reformed Churches Today." In *Reformed Theology in Contemporary Perspective: Westminster: Yesterday, Today —and Tomorrow?*, edited by Lynn Quigley. Edinburgh: Rutherford House, 2006.
Morens, David M., Michael North, and Jeffery K. Taubenberger. "Eyewitness accounts of the 1510 Influenza Pandemic in Europe." *Lancet* 376/9756 (2010) 1894–95.
Moreans, David M., Jeffery K. Taubenberger, Gregory K. Fulkers, and Anthony S. Fauci. "Pandemic Influenza's 500th Anniversary." *Clinical Infectious Diseases* 51/12 (2010) 1442–44.
Nichols, Stephen J. *The Reformation: How a Monk and a Mallet Changed the World*. Wheaton, IL: Crossway, 2007.
Noll, Mark A. "The Earliest Protestants and the Reformation of Education." *Westminster Theological Journal* 43/1 (1980) 97–131.
Ottati, Douglas F. *Theology for Liberal Protestants: God the Creator*. Grand Rapids: Eerdmans, 2013.
Presbyterian Church (USA). *Book of Confessions: Study Edition*. Louisville: Geneva, 1986.
Presbyterian Mission Agency. "The French Confession of 1559." Online: http://www.presbyterianmission.org/ministries/worship/frenchconfession/.
Price, Charles P., and Louis Weil. *Liturgy for Living*. Rev. ed. Harrisburg, PA: Morehouse, 2000.
Ready, Milton. *The Tar Heel State: A History of North Carolina*. Columbia: University of South Carolina Press, 2005.
Rice, Howard L., and James C. Huffstutler. *Reformed Worship*. Louisville: Geneva, 2001.
The Royal Household. "Charles II (r.1660–1685)." The Official Website of the British Monarchy. Online: http://www.royal.gov.uk/HistoryoftheMonarchy/KingsandQueensoftheUnitedKingdom/TheStuarts/CharlesII.aspx.
Schaff, Philip. *Modern Christianity: The Swiss Reformation*. Vol. 13 of *History of the Christian Church*. 1882. Online: http://www.ccel.org/ccel/schaff/hcc8.iv.html.
Skidmore, Chris. *Edward VI: The Lost King of England*. London: Weidenfield and Nicolson, 2007.
Steinmetz, David C. *Reformers in the Wings: From Geiler von Kaysersberg to Theodore Beza*. New York: Oxford University Press, 2001.
Stookey, Laurence Hull. *Eucharist: Christ's Feast with the Church*. Nashville: Abingdon, 1993.
Sunshine, Glenn S. *The Reformation for Armchair Theologians*. Louisville: Westminster John Knox, 2005.
Walker, Williston. *A History of the Christian Church*. Rev. New York: Scribner, 1959.
Way, Peter. "A 'Lutheran' Copy of Erasmus' Edition of St. Augustine." *Lutheran Quarterly* 14 (2000) 372–408.
Weir, Alison. *The Children of Henry VIII*. New York: Ballantine, 1996.

Index

Abelard, Peter, 37
abortion, 25
Act of Supremacy, 91
Act of Uniformity, 93
Address to the Christian Nobility (Luther), 52
Adeodatus (Augustine's son), 31–32
Adrian of Utrecht (Pope Adrian VI), 51–52
Alba, Fernando Álvarez de Toledo, Duke of, 58
Albert of Brandenburg, 48–50
Albertus Magnus, 23
Alexander V, Pope, 36
altars
    Luther's retention of, 53
    replacement with tables, 68, 93–94
    symbolism, 111, 131, 136
Alypius (Augustine's friend), 32
Amadas, Philip, 102
Ambrose, Bishop, 32
Ames, William, 110–11
Amsterdam, the Netherlands, move of Puritans to, 110
Amsdorf, Nikolaus, 57
Anabaptist movement, Anabaptists
    contrasts with Calvinists, 144
    missionary work, 117–18
    persecutions and executions, 66, 117
    precepts, 66, 143, 144
    Schleitheim Confession, 66, 143
Anglicans. *See also* Church of England
    cathedral design, 111
    empowerment under Charles II, 114–15
    support from Mary (wife of William III), 118
    support for James I, 109
    and the Westminster Confession of Faith, 145
Anna of Bohemia (queen of England), 39
Annan, Jacob, 67
Anne of Cleves (sister of the Saxon elector), 91–92
anthropodermic bibiopegy, 29
anti-Semitism. *See* Jews
Aquinas. *See* Thomas Aquinas, Saint
architecture, church
    Anglican cathedrals, Puritan sanctuaries, 111
    impact of Protestant Reformation on, 136
    Roman Catholic, 22
Aristotle, 22, 135
Arminius, 118–19
Articles of Religion (Bucer), 69
Associated Reformed Presbyterian denomination, 112
Atkinson, James, 69–70
atonement, repentance. *See also* election doctrine; the Eucharist; salvation; sinfulness, innate
    in Anabaptist worship, 66
    in Catholic worship, 48
    in the Heidelberg Catechism, 144
    limited, in the TULIP doctrine, 119
Augsburg Confession
    Elizabeth I's affirmation of, 98–99
    Melanchton's presentation of, 58
    precepts in, 143

Index

Augsburg Confession *(cont.)*
    and the Heidelberg Catechism, 60
Augsburg Interim, 58–59
Augustine of Hippo (Saint Augustine)
    on behavior toward Jews, 18
    as bishop of Hippo, 33
    childhood and education, 31–32
    Confessions, 32
    founding of contemplative community, 33
    impact on Roman Catholic worship, 34
    influence on Bradwardine, 36
    influence on Gregory "the Great," 21
    influence on Von Staupitz and Luther, 42
    influence on Wycliffe, 36
    prohibition of divorce, 132–33
    spiritual awakening, 32–33
    theological concepts, 33
Augustinian Protestants, 21, 34
Avicenna, 135

Bacon, Sir Francis, 135
baptism
    adult, 66–67
    baptism through immersion, 111
    the baptismal font, 131, 136
    and development of the English Baptist church, 111
    fees for, 63
    in the French Confession, 124
    infant baptism, 63–64, 66, 143
    James I's requirements concerning, 110
    private and emergency, 110
    and uniting with the Body of Christ, 4, 136
Barlowe, Arthur, 102
Basel, Calvin's settlement in, 73
bath houses, 19
Battle of Tours, 21
Beaton, Cardinal, 105–6
Belgic Confession of Faith, 68, 85, 118, 144
Belgium, establishment of, 118
Benedictine Order, 13, 20

Beneficio di Christo, 3
Bern, Switzerland, Reformed worship in, 75
Bernard of Clairvaux, 37
Beza, Nicolas de, 83
Beza, Pierre de, 83
Beza, Theodore
    career as educator, 78, 83
    childhood and education, 83
    efforts at reconciling Catholic and Protestant theologies, 84
    final years, death and burial, 84
    as headmaster of the Geneva Academy, 83–84
    law practice and spiritual awakening, 83
    personality, 83–84
    portrait, 89
    views on divorce, 133
    writings and translations, 83–84
the Bible. *See* Scripture, the Bible
birth control, Roman Catholic opposition to, 25
bishops
    authority and power, 20, 109, 129
    and the development of the papacy, 21
    encouragement of brothels, 19
    in Lutheran hierarchy, 99
    theological knowledge and conduct, 15, 19
    at Vatican II, 139
Bishop's Bible, 95
the Black Death. *See* bubonic plague ("the Black Death")
Blake, Eugene Carson, 2
"Bloody Mary." *See* Mary Tudor (queen of England)
Bohemia, Reformation in, 39–40
Boleyn, Anne, 90–91
Book of Church Order, 107
Book of Common Order (Kirk), Gaelic translation, 105
Book of Common Prayer
    1549 version, 69, 112
    1552 version, 93–94
    1559 version, 98, 111, 113–14

Index

1662 version, 110
Book of Revelation, Bullinger's commentaries, 65
Bora, Katherine von (wife of Martin Luther), 55, 133
Bourbon, Henry (later Henry XIII, king of France), 121
Bourdelot, Marie, 83
Bowes, Marjorie (wife of John Knox), 106–7
Bradshaw, William, 110
Bradstreet, Anne, 112
Bradwardine, Thomas, 37
bread and wine, sacramental. *See also* the Eucharist
  in Catholic worship, 131
  Christ's presence in, Reformation debates about, 80
  in the French Confession, 124
  receiving of, by the laity, 39–41
  transformation process, 24
  treatment of after celebration, 57
  variable instructions for administering, 81, 93, 110
Brethren of Common Life
  Erasmus's affiliation with, 43
  pragmatism, 44
  as precursor to the Dutch Reformation, 117
brothels
  closing of, in Reformed communities, 75, 132
  encouragement of, by Catholic priests, 19, 132
bubonic plague ("the Black Death")
  and the concept of purgatory, 25
  origins, spread and impacts, 8–11
Bucer, Martin
  anti-Semitism, 69
  Articles of Religion, 69
  childhood and education, 67
  church governance model, 77–78
  as conciliator, bridge-builder, 68–70
  contribution to the Reformed Church, 68–69
  death and reburial, 69, 84
  emphasis on church discipline, 68
  flight to England, 69
  Genevan Psalter, 136
  Luther's influence on, 67
  marriage to Elizabeth Silbereisen, 67
  as mentor to Calvin, 68, 74, 76
  ministry in Landstuhl, 67
  portrait, 87
  Scripture readings, 115
  views on divorce, 133
Bugenhagen, Johannes, 55
Bullinger, Heinrich (Henry)
  commentaries on the Book of Revelation, 65
  leadership of Zurich Reformed church, 65, 84
  perspective on covenant theology, 66
  reforms instituted by, 65–66
  role as educator, 63
  Second Helvetic Confession, 65, 145

Cabot, John, 101
Caffa, Crimea, 8
Cajetan, Cardinal, 50
Calvin (Cauvin), Antoine and Marie, 71
Calvin, John. *See also Christianae Religionis Institutio*
  approach to Jews, 75
  Bible commentaries, 79
  birth, 1, 10
  Bucer's influence on, 74
  celebration of the Lord's Supper, 136
  childhood and education, 71–72
  church offices, 78
  on church's role in discipline, 75
  commentary on Seneca's *De Clementia*, 72
  conflicts with Geneva City Council, 75–77
  death, funeral and burial, 83–84
  definition of the church, 85
  as educator, 30, 77–78
  farewell to Farel, 82–83
  flight from Paris, 73
  Geneva Academy, 78–79
  the Geneva Confession, 75
  Genevan Psalter, 136
  importance of pastoral care to, 79

Index

Calvin, John *(cont.)*
    influence on the Huguenots, 123
    influence on the Scots Confession, 144
    La Forme des Prieres, 107
    leadership of the Geneva Reformed Church, 74, 77–79
    Luther's influence on, 74
    marriage to Idelette de Bure, 76–77
    ministry in Strasbourg, 76
    physical decline, illnesses, 82
    portrait depicting, 88
    on preaching as the Word of God, 81
    preparation for the priesthood, 72
    relationship with Knox, 97, 107
    return to Geneva, 77–78
    sanctification as core precept, 34
    Scripture readings, 115
    small catechism, 105
    as social reformer, 74–75
    spiritual awakening, 71–73
    understanding of the Lord's Supper, 80
    views on divorce, 133
    views on music, 136
    views on soul sleep, 73
    writings, 82–83
Calvinism, Calvinists
    accusations against Frederick III, 60
    conflicts with Lutherans, 144
    and Elizabeth I's inclusive theological approach, 98–99
    the Heidelberg Catechism, 144
    and the Huguenot movement, 120
    in the Netherlands, and the Belgic Confession, 117–18
    radical, expressions of in the Netherlands, 144
    strict, Smyth's rejection of, 110
    the TULIP doctrines, 120
    understanding of grace, 34
Campbell, Archibald (earls of Argyll), 104
capital punishment, Augustine's opposition to, 33
Capuchin Order, founding, 127
Carswell, John, 104–5

Castle Church, Wittenberg, 56, 84
catechisms
    Geneva Catechism, 75, 83, 105
    Heidelberg Catechism, 59–60, 144
    Luther's Small Catechism, 132
    Westminster Confession of Faith and Catechisms, 113, 145
Catherine de' Medici
    assassination of Admiral Coligny, 121
    control over son, Charles IX, 120
    Edict of January, 120
    efforts to curb Protestant power in France, 121
    permission given Huguenots to worship, 84
    reconciliation efforts, 120
Catherine of Aragón (daughter of Ferdinand and Isabella), 90–91
Catherine of Genoa, Saint, 126
Catholic Church. *See also* the papacy, Pope; priests, Catholic
    ambivalence towards women, 132
    Catholic Reformation, 127–29
    Chinese Rites Controversy, 128
    church architecture, 22
    Conciliar Movement and the Great Schism, 35–36
    Council of Trent, 129
    dominance in French rural politics, 120
    enduring loyalty to in Ireland, 114
    growing dysfunctionality, 35
    influence of Augustine on, 33–34
    initial optimism about James I, 109
    the Inquisition, 128
    introduction into Scotland, 104
    liturgy, inclusion in Church of Scotland worship, 110
    Luther's changes to worship and liturgy, 52–53
    monastic orders, 20
    mysticism in, 26
    permission to worship under Elizabeth I, 99
    Pope Paul III's reforms, 126–27
    prohibition of divorce, 132–33
    promotion of poverty as virtue, 132

Index

Regensburg Colloquy, 128
response to Protestant ideas, 130
role in medieval education, 26–27
sale of indulgences, 48–49
in 16th century Spain, 6, 128
Society of Jesus (Jesuits), 127–28
state-controlled in 16th century France, 6
Catholic News Service (USCCB), 29
Catholic worship. *See also* the Eucharist
appeal to the senses, 131
position of Scriptures in devotion, 136
reformation efforts, 35
reforms following Second Vatican Council, 126, 139
service of the Word, 22
transubstantiation, 22
Cauvin, Charles, 71
Cauvin, Gérard and Jeanne Le Franc, 71
Celtic cross, 104
chantry priests, 25, 27
Charles I (king of England)
conflicts with Parliament, 112
defeat by Cromwell, 113
execution, 113
persecution of Puritans, 111
reforms, 112–13
succession, 112
and war between England and Scotland, 112
Charles I (king of Spain, later Emperor Charles V). *See* Charles V (Holy Roman Emperor)
Charles II (king of England), 114
Charles V (Holy Roman Emperor)
abdication, 59
as advisor to Mary Tudor, 96
alliances with Protestants, 143
Augsburg Interim, 58
charges against Frederick III, 60
and the Council of Trent, 128
defeat during second Schmalkadic War, 59
at Diet of Augsburg, 58
election and installation, 51

and the marriage of Henry VIII to Anne Boleyn, 91
and the persecution of Protestants, 117
Charles V (Holy Roman Emperor)
election and installation, 7
land controlled by, 6, 7
Charles VIII (king of France), 6
Charles IX (king of France), 120–21
Charles the Bold, 7
China, Jesuit outreach to, 127–28
Chinese Rites Controversy, 128
Christianae Religionis Institutio (*Institutes of the Christian Religion*) (Calvin)
Calvin's definition of the church in, 85
final edition, 82
importance to the Reformed Church, 74
instructions for administering the Lord's Supper, 80–81
publication and success, 73–74
revisions, 76
church, definition, 68, 85
church calendar, 93, 110
Church of England. *See also* Anglicans; *Book of Common Prayer*
abolition of Episcopal form of church government, 113
Act of Supremacy, 91
Act of Uniformity, 93
Elizabeth I's inclusive theological approach, 98
establishment of Henry VIII as Supreme Head, 91
Forty-Two Articles, 94
marriage service, 94
relationship with James I, 109
revisions to services and practices, 93–94
Thirty-Nine Articles, 98
and the Westminster Confession of Faith, 145
Church of Scotland. *See also* Presbyterianism, Presbyterians
Book of Church Order, 107
emergence, 99–100, 104

Index

Church of Scotland *(cont.)*
    meeting of first General Assembly, 107
    relationship with James I, 110
    Second Book of Discipline, 109
    symbols used in ordination service, 131
    and the Westminster Confession of Faith, 113, 145
Church of St. John the Baptist, Perth, Scotland, 107
churches, local, role in village life, 17
Churches Uniting in Christ (CUIC), 3
church-state separation, Anabaptist and Mennonite views, 66
City of God (Augustine), 33
"On Civil Lordship" (Wycliffe), 37–38
Clement VII, Pope, conflicts with Henry VIII, 90–91
clergy. *See* pastors, ministers; preaching; priests, Catholic
Cloverdale, Myles, 97
COCU (Consultation on Church Union), 2–3
Codex Bezae (Beza), 83–84
Colet, John, 44
Coligny, Admiral Gaspard de, 121
College of France, Paris, 72
collegiums (colleges), 27–28
Colloquy of Poissy, 120
Cologne, Germany, 9
Columba, 104
Columbus, Christopher, 6
Communion service. *See* the Eucharist (Lord's Supper, Communion service)
"Company of Pastors," 83
Conciliar Movement, 35–36
confessional documents, 2. *See also specific confessional documents*
Confessions (Augustine), 32
Congregationalist congregation, 110–11. *See also* Puritan movement
Constance, Council at (1414), 36, 39–40
Consultation on Church Union (COCU), 2–3
convents
    as brothels, 19
    closing of, in Germany, 54, 133
Cop, Nicholas, 72–73
Copernicus, Nicolaus, 134
Cotton, John, 111–12
Council of Trent, 58, 129
"Covenant Relationship between the Korean Church in America and the PC (USA)" (CUIC), 3
covenant theology, 66
craft guilds, 18–19
Cranmer, Thomas (archbishop of Canterbury)
    annulment of Henry VIII's first marriage, 91
    Book of Common Prayer, 69
    changes to Church of England worship, 94
    Forty-Two Articles, 94
    funeral service for Edward VI, 94
    imprisonment and execution, 96–97
Cremova, Gerard, translation of Avicenna's studies, 135
Cromwell, Oliver, 113–15
crop failures, famine, 16
CUIC (Churches Uniting in Christ), 3
Culdees (Servants or Friends of God), 104

da Vinci, Leonardo, 135
de Bure, Idelette (wife of John Calvin), 76–77
De Clementia (On Clemency, Seneca), Calvin's commentary on, 72
de Condé, Louis, 121
de Hangest, Claude, 72
de Vatine, John, 71
deacon's role, Calvin's view, 68, 70, 77–78
demons, body-inhabiting, 25–26
Denosse, Claudine, 83
Diet of Augsburg
    1518, 50
    1530, 143
Diet of Spires, 57–58
Diet of Worms, 52
Directory for Worship (Westminster Assembly), 113

Index

discipline, church
    in Bucer's views on, 68, 85
    Calvin's views on, 75, 77, 85
    in the Church of Scotland, 109, 144
divorce
    and British royal politics, 91–92, 100
    Roman Catholic prohibitions, 132–33
    views on among the various Protestant Reformers, 133
Doctor Faustus (Marlow), 135
doctors, physicians
    in England, impact of the plague, 11
    role of, Calvin's view, 77–78
Dominican Order. *See also* Bucer, Martin; Thomas Aquinas, Saint
    establishment, 126
    poverty and scholarship, 20
    role as traveling preachers, 15
    and the sale of indulgences, 49
    and violence against Jews, 18
double grace, 34
double predestination, 23–24, 145
Douglas, James, 108–9
"Draft Ecclesiastical Ordinances" (Calvin), 77
Dudley, Guilford, 95
Dudley, John (duke of Northumberland), 94–95
Dutch Mennonites, 110
Dutch Reformed Church
    Brethren of Common Life, 117
    debate over predestination, 119–120
    theological decisions following wars with England and Spain, 118–19
Dylan, Bob ("The Times They Are a-Changing"), 142

Early Modern Catholicism, 126–27
Eastern church, monastic orders, 20
Eck, Johann, 51
ecumenical cooperation, 3, 57, 140
Edict of January (Catherine de'Medici), 120
Edict of Nantes, 122–25
education
    availability in medieval Europe, 19, 26–28
    and the clothing of clergy, 131
    humanist systems, 27
    and illiteracy, importance of architecture, 22
    impact of the printing press on, 29–30
    and the "priesthood of all believers," 30
    public school systems, 65
    Reformers' emphasis on, revitalization of, 134–35, 141–42
Edward I (king of England), 18
Edward VI (king of England)
    accession to the throne, 92
    birth, 91
    death, 94
    education, 92
    Knox as chaplain to, 106
    as Protestant supporter, 69, 95
    succession, 95
Edwards, Jonathan, 112
Eisleben, Germany, Luther's death at, 56
elders
    Bucer's views on, 68
    in the Church of Scotland, 107
    in the Geneva Reformed Church, 77–78
election, doctrine of
    Aquinas's teachings, 23–24
    Calvin's acceptance of, 74, 82
    and the concept of double predestination, 23–24
    English Baptist views, 111
    of Huguenots, through suffering, 125
    Puritan views, 125
    unconditional, in TULIP doctrine, 119
    von Staupitz's teachings, 42
    Wtenbogaert's teachings, 119
    Wycliffe's teachings, 38–39
Elizabeth I (queen of England)
    approach to change, 98
    birth, 91
    conflicts with Spain, 99
    education, 133–34
    execution of Mary Stuart, 100
    inclusive theological stance, 98

Index

Elizabeth I (queen of England) *(cont.)*
  Philip II's efforts to marry, 99
  Protestant faith, 97–99
  reburial of Bucer's remains, 69
  relationship with Knox, 106
  succession to the throne, 97
  support for colonization, 102, 114
  as "Supreme Governor" of the Church of England, 98
  Thirty-Nine Articles, 98
emergence concept (Luisi), 137–38
Emmanuel College, 111
England. *See also* Church of England, Parliament *and specific rulers*
  barber-surgeons in, 11–12
  Bucer's sojourn in, 69
  civil war in, 113
  emergence of the Tudor monarchy, 7
  establishment of the Commonwealth, 114–15
  explorations in North America, 102
  plague in, 8, 11
  poor laws, 69
  Spanish efforts to invade, 101
  War of the Roses, 7
  wars with Scotland, 112
English Baptist movement, 110–11
Erasmus, Desiderius
  appointment as secretary to the bishop of Cambrai, 43
  Bachelor of Divinity degree, travels in England, 43
  Brethren of Common Life, 43
  childhood and education, 43–44
  conflicts with Luther, 44
  correspondence with Zwingli, 62
  friendships with Colet and More, 44
  Greek edition of New Testament, 44
  portrait depicting, 86
  pragmatism, 44
  as precursor to Dutch Reformation, 117
  residence in Basel, 73
ethical behavior
  of clergy, and church discipline, 85
  and clergy as moral examples, 66
  Geiler's concept of the moral life, 42
  Melanchthon's differences with Luther over, 57
  and Puritan emphasis on self-examination, 125
  source of in Scripture, 39–40, 48, 135–36
the Eucharist (Lord's Supper, Communion service)
  Aquinas's understanding of, 24
  architecture befitting, 22
  Calvin's understanding and practices for celebrating, 80–81, 136
  celebration of following Vatican II, 139
  celebration of in *The Book of Common Prayer*, 98, 110
  under the Commonwealth, flexibility in worship, 114
  communion tables, 68, 93–94
  conservative challenges to Melanchthon on, 57
  de-emphasis on in Puritan worship, 111
  and excommunication, 17
  as focus in Hussite Church, 40–41
  French king's right to administer, 120
  Luther's changes to, 53
  Puritan practice, 114
  Reform Church changes to celebration of, 136
  replacement of Mass with in Zurich, 63
  revisions to, in England, 93–94, 110
  revisions to in Scotland, 107
  Wycliffe's understanding of, 38
  Zwingli's understanding and practices for celebrating, 63–65, 80
Eugene IV, Pope, 36
evil, 23, 25, 32–33. *See also* sinfulness, innate
excommunication
  in Calvin's Geneva, 75, 77
  by Catholic village priests, impacts, 16–17
  of Henry VIII, 91
  of Luther, 51–52

Index

faith, genuine, overview of Catholic and Protestant perspectives, 34
family life, Reformed Church emphasis on, 132
Farel, Guillaume (William)
    Calvin's farewell note to, 82–83
    childhood and education, 70
    influence of LeFevre, 70
    mentorship of Calvin, 74, 77
    move to Bern, 76
    and the seizure of Catholic Churches in Geneva, 70
    sermon to the Waldensian Synod, 70
Felix V, Pope, 36
Ferdinand (heir of Aragon), 6
Ferdinand (Holy Roman Emperor), 59
"The First Blast of the Trumpet against the Monstrous Regiment of Women" (Knox), 106
folk medicine, 12
forgiveness. *See* justification/forgiveness by faith
"Formula of Agreement between Evangelical Lutheran Church in America, the Presbyterian Church (USA), the Reformed Church in America, and the United Church of Christ" (CUIC), 3
Formula of Concord, 57
"Fort Raleigh" (Roanoke Island), 102–3
Forty-Two Articles (Elizabeth I), 94
Fracastoro, Girolamo, 11
France. *See also* Huguenots *and specific rulers*
    distrust of Protestantism in, 120–21
    foreign conquests, wars with England, 6
    kings, theological dispensations afforded, 120
    plague in, 8
    religious military conflicts, 120
    state-controlled church in, 6
Francis I (king of France)
    dedication of *Christianiae Religionis Instituto* to, 73
    extension of power, 6
    founding of humanist college, 72
    persecution of Lutherans, 73
Francis II (king of France), marriage to Mary Stuart, Queen of Scots, 99, 120
Franciscan Order
    establishment, 126
    opposition to Jesuit practices, 128
    poverty and scholarship, 20
    violent anti-Semitism, 18
Frederick III (emperor of Austria)
    acquittal by the German Diet in 1566, 60
    conversion to Lutheranism and Calvinism, 59
    and the Heidelberg Catechism, 59–60
    Melanchthon as advisor to, 59
    rule over house of Habsburgs, 7
Frederick the Wise, Elector of Saxony
    barring of Dominicans from Saxony, 49
    death and successor, 53
    friendship with von Staupitz, 42
free will, personal choice
    Aquinas's teachings, 23, 25
    and concept of double predestination, 23–24
    Melanchthon's views, 57
    in Wtenbogaert's teachings, 119
French (Gallic) Confession, 123–24, 144
French Revolution, 125
Froment, Antoine, 70
Fust, Johann, 28

Galen, 12, 135
Galileo, 135
galley slaves, slave ships, 106
Garnet, Father Henry (English Jesuit leader), 29
Geddes, Jenny, 112
Geiler von Kayserberg, Johan
    childhood and education, 41
    influence on Melanchthon, 56
    moral reforms, concept of the moral life, 42
    Wycliffe's translation of from Latin, 38

Index

General Baptist congregation, 110
General Synod, Huguenots, 123
Geneva, Switzerland. *See also* Beza, Theodore; Calvin, John; Geneva Academy
    church consistory, 77–78
    church-state power struggles, 75–76
    execution of Servetus, 79–80
    Farels's preaching in, 70
    formal adoption of the Reformed faith, 70
    population decline following Calvin's death, 84
    pressures from Roman Catholic leaders in, 77
    as refuge for persecuted Protestants, 79
    training of French Protestants in, 123
Geneva Academy
    Beza's role as headmaster, 83–84
    founding and curriculum, 78–79
Geneva Confession, Geneva Catechism (Calvin), 75, 83
Genevan Psalter (Calvin and Bucer), 136
George, Duke of Ducal Saxony, 51
Germany, 7–8. *See also* Luther, Martin *and specific German cities and towns*
ghetto, origins of term, 18
ghosts, 25–26
God's love, presence
    in Bucer's teachings, 68
    individuals' ability to experience, 37
    Luther's direct experience of, 45, 47–48
    in Porphyry's teachings, 32
    in Von Staupitz's teachings, 42
    in Wtenbogaert's teachings, 119
Gonzalez, Justo, 35
Gormarus, Franciscus, 119
Gottfried, Robert, 12
grace, God's. *See also* the Eucharist; salvation
    Bradwardine's teachings, 37
    double grace, 34
    in the French Confession, 123–24
    in Geiler's preaching, 42

irresistible grace, 33–34, 119
    and justification by faith, 73–74
    Lutheran vs. Calvinist perspectives, 34
    Luther's conflicts with the pope over, 48
    Luther's teachings, 48
    Roman Catholic *vs.* Protestant views on, 34
    Wtenbogaert's teachings, 119
Great Bible translation (Coverdale), 110
Great Cathedral, Zurich, 62
Great Saint Mary's Church, Cambridge, England, 69
Great Schism, 36
Grebel, Conrad, 66
Greek. *See* Latin and Greek
Greenville, Richard, 102–3
Gregory "the Great" (bishop of Rome)
    concept of purgatory, 24
    rule, 35
    theological assertions, 21
Grey, Lady Jane, 95
Groote, Gerhard, 43
Gunpowder Plot, implication of Jesuits in, 29
Gutenberg, Johann, 28

Habsburg, House of, 7, 135
Hamilton, Patrick, 104–105
Harvey, William, 12, 135
heaven
    Catholic views, 132
    and the Lord's Supper, 64, 80
    Platonist views, 24–25
    and purgatory, 25–26
Hebrew Bible studies, 62, 73, 75
Hebrew grammar (Reuchlin), 43
The Heidelberg Catechism
    consequences, 60
    precepts, 144
    writing, adoption and revision, 59–60
Helwys, Thomas, 110
Henry Bourbon (later Henry IV), 122
Henry II (king of France), 59, 120
Henry III (king of France), persecution of Huguenots, 121–22

Index

Henry IV (king of England), persecution of Lollards, 38
Henry IV (king of France). *See* Henry Bourbon
Henry V (king of England)
    execution of leader of the Lollards, 39
    founding of the College of Medicine and the Fellowship of Surgeons, 12
Henry VII (king of England)
    as absolute ruler, 7
    and ascension of Tudors to the British throne, 39
    effort to marry son Arthur to Catherine of Aragon, 90
    and John Cabot's explorations of North America, 101
Henry VIII (king of England)
    Calvin's funeral sermon, 83
    and emergence of state-controlled church in England, 7
    establishment as Supreme Head of the Church of England, 91
    excommunication, 91
    founding of the Royal College of Physicians, 12
    marriage to Catherine Howard, 92
    marriage to Catherine of Aragon, 90
    marriage to Catherine Parr, 92
    marriage to Jane Seymour, 91
Henry of Guise, 122
Hepburn, James (lord of Bothell), 100
Highland Scots, Protestant clans, 104
Hippocrates, 12
hired hands (*journalists*), 15
Holy Spirit. *See also* God's love, presence
    as active in church life, Zwingli's views, 62
    ministers as voices for, Anabaptist view, 66
    ministers as voices for, Calvin's view, 81–82
    revelation of in Scripture, as key to Reformation theology, 4, 119, 123–24, 136, 141
Hooker, Thomas, 111
Howard, Catherine, 92
Huguenot movement, Huguenots
    and the Edict of January, 120
    growth and influence, 123–25
    influence of Calvin on, 123
    loss of influence and power, 126
    under Louis XIII, 122
    peace treaty with, 120
    permission to worship in France, 84, 121–22
    persecution, 120, 125
    St. Bartholomew Day's Massacre, 121
humanism. *See also* Erasmus, Desiderius
    humanist educational systems, 27
    influence of Calvin, 72–73, 75
    influence on Farel, 70
    influence on modern theology, 130, 132, 134
    influence on Zwingli, 61–62
Huss, John
    branding as heretic, 36, 40
    childhood and education, 39
    excommunication, 39–40
    imprisonment and execution, 40, 51
    nationalism, 39
    theological reforms, 39
Hussite Church, 40–41
Hutter, Jacob, Hutterites, 66–67

Index of Prohibited Books, 42, 128
indulgences, selling of, 48–50
infant baptism, debates about, 63–64, 66, 143. *See also* baptism
infection, as a concept, 11
influenza pandemics, 10–11
Iona, Scotland, 104
Ireland, 114
irresistible grace, 21, 33, 119
Isabella (heir of Castile), 6
Islam, Muslims
    conquests by, impact on European Christianity, 21
    scientific discoveries, 135
    targeting during Spanish Inquisition, 128
Italy
    ghettoes, 18
    and the Oratory of Divine Love, 126
    plague in, 8

Index

Jacobs, Henry, 110
James I (king of England, also James VI of Scotland)
  birth, 100
  and the Gunpowder plot, 29
  as king of England and Scotland, 109
  and the settlement of Jamestown, 102
  Ulster Plantation, 114
James I (king of England and Scotland)
  changes to Church of England worship, 109–10
  coronation as James VI of Scotland, 100
  reign over Scotland, 109
James VI (king of Scotland). *See* James I (king of England, also James VI of Scotland)
Jamestown, Virginia, 103
Japan, 2011 earthquake and tsunami, 5
Jerome of Prague, 40
Jesus, as a prophet, 79
Jews
  Augustine's views, 18
  blame and punishment for plague, 9
  Bucer's prejudice against, 69
  Calvin's views, 75
  expulsion from England, 18
  Luther's prejudice against, 55–56
  persecution, 9
  return to England under Cromwell, 115
  targeting during Spanish Inquisition, 128
"On Jews and Their Lies" (Luther), 55
John "the Steadfast," Elector of Saxony, 53
John XXII, Pope (20th century)
  canonization of Thomas Aquinas, 23
  Second Vatican Council, 139
John XXIII, Pope (15th century), 36
Juana (daughter of Ferdinand and Isabella), 7
Julius II, Pope, 11
justification/forgiveness by faith. *See also* the Eucharist
  Calvin's teachings, 34, 73–74
  in Catholic worship, 34, 129
  in Lutheran worship, 34

Melanchthon's teachings, 57

Karlstadt, Andreas Bodenstein von, 51, 52–53
Kearny, John, 114
Killigrew, Sir Henry, 108
King James Bible, 110
kneeling, changing interpretations of, 94
Knox, John
  attacks on Mary Stuart, 100
  birth and education, 105
  "Black Rubric," 94
  and the *Book of Church Order*, 107
  branding as "outlaw," 107
  as chaplain to Edward VI, 106
  at coronation of James VI of Scotland, 100
  final sermon, death and burial, 108
  "The First Blast of the Trumpet against the Monstrous Regiment of Women," 106
  flight from Scotland, 97
  as a galley slave, 106
  help with the Geneva Bible, 97
  marriage to Margaret Stewart, children, 107–8
  marriage to Marjorie Bowes, 106
  ordination and work as tutor, 105
  portrait depicting, 89
  The Scots Confession, 144
  sermons, incendiary nature of, 107
  stroke and other illnesses, 108
  support for Protestant rebels, 105–6
Knox, William, 105
Kotter, John P., 140–41

La Forme des Prieres (Calvin), 107
laboreurs, 15
land owners
  absent, notaries as representatives of, 16
  criticisms of by traveling friars, 20
  educational opportunities, 26–27
  and tenant farming, 15
Landstuhl, Switzerland, 67
Latimer, Bishop Hugh, 96
Latin and Greek

Index

Elizabeth I's knowledge of, 97–98
Erasmus's studies, 44, 62–63
Gutenberg's Bible, 28
as languages of scholarship, 26–27
the Latin Mass in, and rote recitation, 15
Latin Vulgate, 35, 38
preaching in, rejection by Reformers, 93, 136
studies of, by Reformed leaders, 73, 83
Latin School of St. George (Eisenach, Germany), 46
Laud, William (Archbishop of Canterbury), 112–13
Lausanne academy, 83
law, development as a profession, 27
leadership, management vs., 141
lectionary
    Bucer's replacement with full Gospel, 68
    1549 version, omission of Book of Revelation, 65
    Vatican II reforms, 139
    Zwingli's replacement with readings from the New Testament, 62, 65
LeFèvre d'Etaples, Jacques, 70, 73
Leipzig, Germany, 51
Leipzig Interim, 59
Leith, John H., 81–82
Leo X, Pope
    death, 51
    Diet of Augsburg, 50
    excommunication of Luther, 50–51
    selling of indulgences, 48–49
Leyden, the Netherlands, 111
liturgical year, discontinuance, 68
Loci Communes (Melanchthon), 57
Lollard movement, Lollards, 38–39
London, plague in, 8
Long Parliament, 113
Lord's Prayer
    in devotions of Order of Saint Bridget of Sweden, 26
    in the Heidelberg Catechism, 144
    Luther's paraphrasing, 53
Lords Supper. *See* the Eucharist

Louis XI (king of France), 6–7
Louis XII (king of France), 6, 10–11
Louis XIII (king of France), 122
Louis XIV (king of France), 125
love. *See* God's love, presence
Lowland Scots, 104. *See also* Knox, John
Loyola, Ignatius, 127
Luisi, Pier Luigi, 138
Luther, Hans, 46–47
Luther, Martin
    Address to the Christian Nobility, 52
    advocacy of female literacy, 133
    agreement with Pope Leo X, 51
    anti-Semitism, 55
    appointment to University of Wittenberg faculty, 49
    beer consumption, 47
    childhood and education, 46–47
    concept of "soul sleep," 25
    conflicts with Erasmus, 44
    and the cult of Saint Ann, 26
    death, funeral and burial, 56
    and destruction of shrines to the Virgin Mary, 52
    and the Diet of Augsburg, 1518, 50
    emotional struggles, 46, 47
    excommunication, 51–52
    and the 1519 Leipzig debate, 51
    friendship with Melanchthon, 57
    health problems, 55
    in hiding at Wartburg Castle, Eisenach, 52
    influence on Bucer, 67
    influence on Calvin, 74
    instructions regarding worship, 53
    lectures on the Psalms, 47
    love for music, 46
    marriage to Katherine von Bora, 55
    and modern-day divisions among Reformed Churches, 3
    Ninety-Five Theses, 49
    opposition to the Peasant's Revolt, 53
    ordination, 47
    as part of the medieval world, 137
    personality, 55
    portrait depicting, 86
    refusal to recant, 52

Index

Luther, Martin *(cont.)*
    response to Copernicus, 134
    on sexual behavior of cardinals, 19
    spiritual/theological insights, 47–48, 56, 64, 143
    spiritual transformation, 45, 47
    support for infant baptism, 63–64
    Von Staupitz's mentorship of/loyalty to, 42
Lutheranism, Lutherans
    attacks on Melanchthon, 57
    and the closure of monasteries around Wittenberg, 53–54
    and Elizabeth I's affirmation of the Augsburg Confession, 99
    The Formula of Concord, 57
    Frederick III and Maria of Brandenburg-Kulmbach, 59
    the Heidelberg Catechism, 144
    as heretics, 145
    missionary work, 117
    and the Peace of Augsburg, 59
    persecution of in France, 73
    understanding of grace, 34

Madgeburg, Germany, school, 46
Mainz, Germany, 9, 48–49
Major, Patrick, 105
Malcolm III (king of Scotland), 104
management, leadership *vs.*, 141
Manichaeism, 32
Mansfield, Germany, 46
manuscripts, hand-copied, 29
Margaret (queen of Scotland), 104
Maria of Brandenburg-Kulmbach (wife of Frederick III), 59
Marlow, Christopher (*Doctor Faustus*), 135
marriage
    and annulment in the Catholic church, 133
    arranged, 18–19
    as economic decision, 14
    impact of Protestant Reformation, 132
    service for, in the *Book of Common Prayer*, 94

The Marrow of Theology (Ames), 111
Marshall, Peter, 45
Martel, Charles, 21
Martin V, Pope
    election at Council of Constance, 36
    excommunication of Huss, 39–40
Martyr, Peter, 97
Mary (daughter of Charles the Bold), 7
Mary (wife of William III), 118
Mary of Guise (regent of Scotland)
    as ruler of Scotland, 99
    and the seizure and punishment of Knox, 105–6
Mary Stuart (Queen of Scots)
    execution, 100
    Knox's criticisms of, 100
    marriage to Francis II of France, 99
    marriage to Henry Stuart, 100
    relationship with James Hepburn, 100
    return to Scotland, 99–100
    son (later James I), 100
    turn towards Protestantism, 100
Mary Tudor (queen of England)
    birth, 90
    as "Bloody Mary," 96
    burning of Bucer's bones, 69
    changes to Church of England worship, 96
    and the execution of Lady Jane Grey, 95
    execution of Thomas Cranmer, 91
    and flight of Protestants to Zurich, 65
    marriage to Philip II of Spain, 96
    as successor to Edward VI, 95–96
Mass, Roman Catholic. *See also* the Eucharist
    Bucer's substituting Lords Supper for, 68
    Latin, rationale for, 15
    Luther's changes to, 53
    Vatican II reforms, 139
Massachusetts Colony, 111
Mather, Cotton and Increase, 111
Matthew 27:25, Calvin's commentary on, 75
Maximilian (Holy Roman Emperor), 50–51

Index

Maximilian I (Emperor of Austria), 7
Mayflower (ship), 111
medical practice
    development as a profession, 27
    folk medicine, 12–13
    Greek traditions, 12–13
    impact of plague on, 8
    in medieval England, 11–12
Melanchthon, Philip
    as advisor to Frederick III, 59
    the Augsburg Confession, 58, 143
    belief in ghosts and demons, 25–26
    challenges to by conservative Lutherans, 57
    childhood and education, 56
    on church's role in developing ethics, 57
    death and burial, 84
    educational reforms, 30
    eulogy at Luther's funeral, 56
    friendship with Luther, 57
    portrait depicting, 88
    views on divorce, 133
Melville, Andrew, 109
Mennonite movement, 66
ministers. *See* pastors, ministers, Reformed clergy
monastic orders, convents
    closing of, impacts on women, 133
    community service, 20
    as keepers of the Christian faith, 35
    role in medieval education, 26–27
    role in providing political stability, 20
    theological scholasticism, 22
Moors, 6
Moravian Brethren, 41
More, Sir Thomas, 44, 91
Morning Prayer and Sermon, 69
Morton, John, 110
Motterwitz, Germany, 42
"Against the Murderous and Thieving Rabble of the Peasants" (Luther), 53
music
    during worship, Reform view as idolatrous, 63, 131
    as conveyer of faith, 46, 136

mysticism, Catholic, 26

National Covenant (1638), 112
Nazi Kristallnacht, 55–56
Neo-Platonic philosophy, 23–24, 32–33
the Netherlands
    Brethren of Common Life, 43
    diversity of worship in, 118
    early Protestant Reform movements in, 117, 118
    freedom of worship in, 118
    identification of Protestant struggle with political struggle against King Phillip II of Spain, 144
    loss of Protestant influence in, 126
    and Philip II's reign, 118
    William of Orange and the partition of the country, 118
New Testament. *See also* Scripture, the Bible
    and Bucer's functions of the ministry, 69
    Bullinger's commentaries on, 62
    Calvin's French translation, 83
    Codex Bezae, 84
    English translations, 38
    Erasmus's Greek and Latin translations, 62
    Greek, Beza's annotations, 83
    Greek, Elizabeth I's reading of, 97–98
    Greek, Erasmus's publication of, 44
    Latin translation, Erasmus's publication and dissemination of, 44
    Zwingli's replacement of lectionary with, 62
New World explorations, 101–2
Nicene Creed, 33
Ninety-Five Theses (Luther), 6, 49–50, 139
nobility, medieval, 13–14
North America, European explorations of, 101
notaries, 15, 16, 71, 106
Noyon, France, 72

offertory
    Bucer's replacement with "self-sacrifice," 69
    Luther's elimination of, 53
Old Celtic Church, 104
Old Testament, Bullinger's commentaries on, 65. *See also* Scripture, the Bible
Olevianus, Casper, 59, 144
Oratory of Divine Love, 126
Order of the Hermits of Saint Augustine, 42, 47, 50
Order of Saint Bridget of Sweden, 26
original sin. *See* sinfulness, innate
Osiander, Andreas, 57
Ottati, Douglas
    on Augustine's doctrine in Roman Catholic church practice, 34
    on differences between Lutheran and Calvinist understandings of grace, 34
    on Luisi's "emergence" scenario, application to Reform, 137–38
Oxford University, 27, 116

pacifism, Anabaptist and Mennonite adherence to, 66–67
Palatinate ruler, 144
papacy, popes. *See also* Catholic Church
    Aquinas's commitment to, 25
    and the Conciliar Movement, 35–36
    role in providing stability to medieval society, 21
    strengthening of by the Council of Trent, 129
    supremacy of, 36
paper, writing, 28
Paré, Ambrose, 135
Paris, France, 8, 123. *See also* University of Paris
Parliament, English. *See also* Church of England
    Act of Supremacy, 91
    Act of Uniformity, 93
    conflicts with Charles I, 112–13
    conflicts with Cromwell, 113
    strengthening of during War of the Roses, 7
    Westminster Confession of Faith and Catechism, 145
Parr, Catherine, 92
pastors, ministers, Reformed clergy. *See also* priests, Catholic
    Anabaptist rejection of education for, 66
    clothing, 131
    "Company of Pastors," 83
    education, 131
    from France, studies in Geneva, 123
    Lollard, exclusion from public office, 38
    priests as, 129
    role of, Bucer's view, 68
    role of, Calvin's view, 77–78
    selection of by congregation, 54
    transformation of studies into offices, 142
Pater, Walter, 135
Paul III, Pope
    recognition of the Society of Jesus, 127
    reforms to the Roman Catholic church, 126
    Roman Inquisition, 128
Paul IV, Pope
    continuation of inquisition policies, 128
    and the Council of Trent, 129
    Index of Prohibited Books, 42, 128
Pavia, Council at, 36
Peace of Augsburg, 59
peasants. *See also* village society
    family isolation, 16
    Peasants Revolts, 38, 53
Pelagius, 33
Perth, Scotland, 107
Philip (son of Mary and Maximilian I), 7
Philip II (king of Spain)
    ascension to throne of the Netherlands, 117
    brutality towards Protestants, 117
    efforts to marry Elizabeth I and conquer England, 99

Index

marriage to Mary Tudor, 96
and Protestant struggles in the Netherlands, 144
response to Mary Stuart's execution, 100–101
territories ruled by, 59
Pike, Bishop James, 2–3
pipe organs, 63, 131
Plato, 24
Plymouth Colony, 111
pneumonic plague, 8
Poissy, France, 84
Porphyry, 32
poverty, the poor
   Elizabethan poor laws, 69
   in medieval Europe, 16–17
   monastic poverty, 20, 132
   Reform views on, 78, 93, 107, 124, 132
   Society of Jesus (Jesuits), 127
Prague, Bohemia, 39
preaching. *See also* pastors, minister, Reformed clergy
   Bible-based, need for reemphasis on, 141–42
   Catholic prohibitions against, 117
   as communicating Word of God and voice of the Holy Spirit, 68, 78, 81–82, 85, 136–37, 141, 144
   focus on within the Reformed movement, 63, 65, 80–81, 83, 111, 131–32, 139–40
predestination. *See also* election doctrine; salvation
   Aquinas's teachings on, 23–24
   Augustine's teachings on, 33
   Bradwardine's teachings on, 37
   debates in the Dutch Reformed Church about, 119–120
   double predestination, 23–24, 145
   emphasis on in the TULIP doctrines, 119
   Gregory the Great's view on, 21
   Melanchton's and Luther's differing views of, 57
   in the Westminster Confession, 145
   Wtenbogaert's teachings on, 119
Presbyterianism, Presbyterians. *See also* Church of Scotland
   under Cromwell, 113–14
   initial support for James I, 109
   missionary work, 104
   National Covenant, 112
   ordination service, 131
   reaction to Charles I's religious mandates, 112
   Second Book of Discipline, 109
   support for Charles I, 113
   and the Ulster Plantation, 114
presbyteries, 109–10, 131
priesthood of all believers, 30
priests, Catholic. *See also* pastors, ministers, Reformed clergy
   Bucer's substituting parson/minister for, 68
   chantry priests, 25, 27
   criticisms of by traveling friars, 20
   exemption from taxes, rationale for, 13
   lack of education, 15
   Morning Prayer and Sermon, 69
   power of excommunication, 16
   reform efforts, 127, 131
   support of through tithes, resistance to, 13
   status in village society, 15
   traveling friars, 20
   use of brothels, 19
printing press
   and the dissemination of Erasmus's writings, 44
   and the dissemination of Luther's Ninety-Five Theses, 49–50
   in England, government control over, 139
   in Germany, number of, 49, 139
   invention of, impacts, 28–30
   and the King James Bible, 110
   and the sharing of knowledge and ideas, 11
privateers, 99, 101
prostitution, 19, 75
Protestant Episcopal Church, 3

Index

Protestant Reformation. *See also* Reformed Church *and specific denominations, reformers and locations*
   and the Catholic Reformation, 130
   and the emergence of Early Modern Europe, 137
   emphasis on education and the sciences, 134–36
   as an example of emergence, 138–39
   factors leading to, importance of understanding, 4
   impact on women, 132
   influence of humanism on, 25, 44
   need to re-embrace heritage from, 130, 140
   origins of term, 58
   persecutions associated with, 38–39, 41, 66, 73, 130, 134
   as providential, 3–6, 139
   timeline of events associated with, 146–152
Psalms, 47, 136
Psalters
   Coverdale's Great Bible translation, 110
   the Genevan Psalter, 136
   Mainz Psalter, 30
Psychopannychia (Calvin), 73
pulpits
   in Church of England sanctuaries, 94
   conduct of services from, 107
   first appearance of in Catholic churches, 22
   focus on, in Reformed sanctuaries, 111, 131, 136
purgatory
   belief in, and Masses for the dead, 25
   and double predestination, 23–24
   and Roman Catholic mysticism, 25–26
   and the sale of indulgences, 48–49
   soul sleep vs., 25
Puritan movement, Puritans
   Bucer's criticisms, 69
   colonies in New England, 111
   Congregationalists and English Baptists, 110–11
   importance of education to, 111
   move to Amsterdam, 110
   religious practices, 114, 125
   sanctuary design, 111
   separation from Church of England, 110–11
   and the Westminster Confession of Faith, 145

Raleigh, Sir Walter, 102–3
"Ralph Lane Colony," 102
rape, as means of power, 19
Raynal, Charles E. III, 78–79
Reformed Church. *See also* the Protestant Reformation; Reformed worship *and specific denominations, countries and reformers*
   Augustinian Protestants, 21, 34
   during the late 16th century, 126
   influence of Vatican II on, 138–140
   in Ireland, 115
   modern challenges and needs, 140–41
   strength during the 16th century, 2
   in Wales, 116
   in Zurich, 63–64
Reformed Congregation of the Hermits of Saint Augustine, 42
Reformed worship. *See also* the Eucharist; preaching, Protestant Reformation; Scripture *and individual denominations and reformers*
   Bucer's contributions to, 68–69
   Bullinger's contributions to, 145
   Calvin's contributions to, 74–75, 80–81
   Church of England, 93–95, 114–15
   Church of Scotland, 107, 110
   comparisons with Catholic worship, 131
   Luther's contributions to, 53, 57, 63–64
   Puritan practice, 111, 113
   sanctuary design, 136

and services in the language of the
people, 39
TULIP doctrines, 119–120
Wtenbogaert's contributions to, 119
Zwingli's contributions to, 63–65, 80
Regensburg Colloquy, 128
Reinhart, Anna (wife of John Zwingli), 62
renters (*laccataires*), rentiers, 15, 19
Reuchlin, Johann (also Johannes), 43, 56
On the Revolution of Celestial Spheres (Copernicus), 134
Richard III (king of England), 39
Richelieu, Cardinal Armand Jean du Plessis, 122
Ridley, Nicholas, 96
Roanoke Island, Virginia, 102–3
Roman Catholic Church. *See* Catholic Church; Catholic worship
Roman Inquisition, 128
Romans 1:17, and Luther's spiritual insights, 47–48
Romans 11:28-32, Calvin's commentary on, 75
Romans 13:13-14, and Augustine's spiritual awakening, 32
Rosary, origins of, 26
Rump Parliament, 113

Saint Andrews, Scotland, 104
Saint Ann, cult of, 26
Saint-Germain-en-Laye, France, 120
salvation. *See also* election
and indulgences, 48
Bradwardine's teachings, 37
through Catholic priests' sacrifices, 13
in the French Confession, 123
role of free will, 57
through subjection to the pope, 25
and the transformation of society, 132
in the TULIP doctrine, 119
and unconditional election, 42
in Wtenbogaert's teachings, 118–19
Zwingli's conflicts with Luther over, 64
sanctification (spiritual renewal), 34
Saxony, barring of Dominicans, 49

Schaffhausen, Switzerland, 41
The Schleitheim Confession, 66, 143
Schmalkaldic League, 58–59
Schmalkaldic War, Second, 59
Schöffer, Peter, 28
scholasticism, theological, 22–24
Schott, Peter, 41
Schwabach Articles (Luther), 143
scientific inquiry
Augustine's support for, 34
and the Protestant Reformation, 134–35
Scotland. *See also* Church of Scotland; Presbyterianism, Presbyterians
British rule over, 109
Cromwell's conquest, 114
formal adoption of Reformed faith, 107
Lowland (English) *vs.* Highland (Gaelic), 104
Old Celtic Church, 104
origins of Christianity in, 104
war with England over Charles I's reforms, 112
The Scots Confession
adoption of by Scottish Parliament, 107
content, 144
inclusion of Bucer's mark of discipline in, 68, 85
Scripta Anglicana (Bucer), 68, 85
Scripture, the Bible. *See also* New Testament; preaching
Abelard's use of reason to understand, 37
allegorical interpretations, 32
Anabaptist interpretation, 143
as authoritative (direct Word of God) in matters of faith and conduct, 34, 38–40, 81, 136, 141–42
the Bishop's Bible, 95
Calvin's commentaries on, 79, 83
central position in Puritan sanctuaries, 111
daily devotional readings, 43
and debates about infant baptism, 66
early commentaries on, 35

Scripture, the Bible *(cont.)*
　English translations, 38
　as focus, in Reformed worship, 77, 81, 111, 115, 131–32, 134, 136, 141
　the Geneva Bible, 97
　the Great Bible, 110
　Greek and Hebrew, reformers studies of, 3, 18, 42–43, 62, 73, 75, 78
　the King James Bible, 110
　Latin Vulgate, 35, 38
　Luther studies and understanding of importance of, 47–48, 52, 60, 133
　modern need to emphasize, 141–42
　monastic interpretations, 35
　preaching using, and the development of the pulpit, 22
　Puritan commentaries on, 111
　role in Catholic worship, 136
　role in Church of England worship, 93–94, 114–15
　role in Church of Scotland worship, 107
　as source of truth, Council of Trent view, 129
　static interpretation during decades following fall of Rome, 35
　translation into Welsh, 116
　Wycliffe's views on fundamental importance, 38
　Zwingli's views on fundamental importance, 62–63, 65
Second Book of Discipline (Scottish General Assembly), 109
the Second Coming
　Augustine's views, 18
　Bullinger's views, 65–66
　and purgatory, 25
　and soul sleep, 25
Second Diet of Spires, 58
The Second Helvetic Confession, 65, 145
Second Vatican Council (Vatican II) reforms, 129, 139
Servetus, Miguel, 79–80
sexuality
　Aquinas's struggles with/writings on, 22–23, 25
　Augustine's struggles with, 31, 32

　Roman Catholic *vs.* Protestant attitudes towards, 132
Seymour, Edward, 92–94
Seymour, Jane, 91
Short Parliament, 113
shrines
　Luther's call for destruction of, 52
　pilgrimages to, rejection by Lollards, 38
　as sources of spiritual comfort, 26
Sigismund (king of Hungary, Holy Roman Emperor), 36, 39–40
Silbereisen, Elizabeth (wife of Martin Bucer), 67
Simons, Menno, 66
sinfulness, innate. *See also* atonement, repentance; the elect; salvation
　Augustinian Protestant views, 34
　Augustine's views on, 33–34
　as cause of illness, 11
　and concept of purgatory, 21, 24
　and indulgences, 48
　Pelagius's teachings, 33
　Roman Catholic views on, 34
　in TULIP doctrine, 119
　in von Staupitz's teachings, 42
　in Wtenbogaert's teachings, 119
slavery
　Augustine's opposition to, 33
　galley slaves, slave ships, 106
Small Catechism (Luther), 132
Smyth, John, 110
Society of Jesus (Jesuits), 127–28
soul sleep, 25, 73
sounding boards, 111, 131
Southwick, England, 110–11
Spain. *See also* Philip II (king of Spain)
　emergence as world power, 6
　relationship of church and state in, 6
　the Spanish Armada, 101
　the Spanish Inquisition, 128
St. Andrews College, 105
St. Bartholomew Day's Massacre, 121
St. Giles Church, Edinburgh, 108, 112
St. Peter's Basilica, building of, 49
St. Peter's Cathedral, Geneva, 74, 84

Index

stewardship, faithful, Wycliffe's concept, 37
Stewart, Margaret (wife of John Knox), 107
Strasbourg (Alsace)
    Bucer's ministry in, 67–69
    Calvin's ministry in, 76–77, 79
    formal adoption of Calvinism, 70
    Geisler's ministry in, 41–42
    massacre of Jews in, 9
    as sanctuary for Beccon and Martyr, 97
On the Structure of the Human Body (Vesalius), 135
Stuart, Henry (Lord Darnley), 100
Stuart, James (early of Morey), 99
Summa Theologiae (Thomas Aquinas), 23–24
surgeons/barber-surgeons, 11–12
Swiss Brethren, 67, 143
Switzerland, persecution of Anabaptists, 66. *See also specific denominations and individuals*
Synod of Dort, 119
Synod of Waldenses, 70
syphilis, 10

tax structures, medieval, 13, 19
Tempier, Stephen (archbishop of Paris), 23
tenant farmers, 15
Tetzel, Johan (Dominican monk), 49
Thagaste, North Africa, 31, 33
Theatines, 127
Theology for Liberal Protestants (Ottati), 137–38
Thirty Years' War, 122
Thirty-Nine Articles (Elizabeth I), 98
Thomas Aquinas, Saint
    biographical sketch, 22–23, 25
    Greek and Islamic influences on, 23
    and prohibition of divorce, 133
    Summa Theologiae, 23–24
    theological concepts, 25
    understanding of the Eucharist, 24
Throckmorton, Nicholas, 97–98
tithes, 13, 15

Torgau Articles (Luther), 143
transubstantiation, doctrine of. *See also* the Eucharist
    Aquinas's teachings, 24
    Catholic reaffirmation for, 129
    and church architecture, 22
    influence among Christians in Bohemia, 39
    Mennonite disagreement with, 66
    rejection of by Lollards, 38
    Wycliffe's attacks on, 38
Triers, 114
Trinity, doctrine of. *See also* Holy Spirit
    Augustine's understanding, 33
    discussion of in the Belgic Confession, 144
    Servetus's rejection of, implications, 79–80
true church, definition in the Scots Confession, 144
TULIP doctrines (Dutch Reformed Church), 119–120
Tyndale, William, 25

Ulster Plantation, 114
United Presbyterian Church USA, 2
University of Basel, 61
University of Bologna, 27
University of Bourges, 72, 74–75
University of Cambridge
    Beza's presentation of *Codex Bezae* to, 84
    Bucer's teaching position at, 69
    school founded by Puritans at, 111
University of Cologne, 23
University of Erfurt, 47
University of Freiburg, 41
University of Heidelberg, 84
University of Leipzig, 39
University of Leyden, 118
University of Naples, 22
University of Orleans
    Beza's studies at, 83
    Calvin's studies at, 72
University of Paris
    Aquinas's teaching position at, 23
    Calvin's studies at, 72

Index

University of Paris *(cont.)*
    Loyola's studies at, 127
    Reuchlin's studies at, 43
    theological approach, 120
University of Prague, 39
University of Salerno, 27
University of Tubingen, 56
University of Vienna, 61
University of Wittenberg
    founding, 42
    Luther's studies at, 47
    Luther's teaching position at, 49
    Melanchthon's teaching position at, 56
    von Staupitz's teaching position at, 42
urban society during the middle ages, 17–19, 27–28, 30
Ursinus, Zacharius, 59, 144

Valerius, bishop of Hippo, 33
Vasquez de Aylon, Luis, 102
Vatican II. *See* Second Vatican Council
Verrazano, Giovanni de, 102
Vesalius, Andreas (*On the Structure of the Human Body*), 135
vestments, Catholic, Bucer's abolition of, 68
village society during the middle ages, 14–17
Viret, Pierre, 83
Virgin Mary, cult of, 26
Virginia, British colonization, 102–3
"Visible Marks of Churches Uniting in Christ" (CUIC), 3
von Sickingen, Franz, 67
Von Staupitz, Johannes, 39, 42. *See also* Lollards

Wales, Reformation movement in, 116
war, just vs. unjust, 25
Weekly Communion, 69
Wesley, John, 41
Westminster Assembly, 113
The Westminster Confession of Faith and Catechisms, 2, 113, 166-169, 145
Westminster Directory for Worship, 114–15

White, John, 103
Whitford, Bishop Walter, 112
Wildhaus, Switzerland, 61
William III (Prince of Orange), 118
wine. *See* bread and wine, sacramental
Winthrop, John, 111
Wishart, George, 105
witchcraft persecutions, 134
Wittenberg, Germany. *See also* Luther, Martin; University of Wittenberg
    during the 16th century, 47
    closure of monasteries in, 53–54
women
    and the closing of convents, 133
    and divorce, 132–33
    Luther's views on, 133
    Protestant, execution and persecution of, 133
    single, unmarried, limits on, 18–19
    witchcraft persecutions, 134
Wurzburg, Germany, 41
Wycliffe, John
    branding as heretic, 38
    challenges to church authority, 37
    death and burials, 38
    influence on Huss, 39
    influence on the Lollard movement, 38–39
    theological teachings, 37–38

yeomen, 15

Zizka, Jan ("One-Eyed Jack"), 41
Zurich, Switzerland
    city council approval of Zwingli's proposals for church reformation in, 63
    defeat at Battle of Kappel, 65
    persecution and execution of Anabaptists in, 66
    Zwingli's ministry in, 61–62
Zurich Reformed church, 63–64, 84
Zwingli, Huldrych (Ulrich)
    academy founded by, 63
    as chaplain to the Swiss military, 61–62
    childhood and education, 61

Index

contributions to the Reformed
  Church, 65, 118, 143
correspondence with Erasmus, 62
death, 65
differences with Luther, 64
educational reforms, 30
influences on, 62
marriage to Anna Reinhart, 62

portrait depicting, 87
and Scripture-based religious
  practice, 63
support for infant baptism, 63–64
theological studies, ordination, 61
theological views, 62–63, 65, 80, 133
Zwingli, Ulrich and Margaretha, 61

www.ingramcontent.com/pod-product-compliance
Lightning Source LLC
Chambersburg PA
CBHW071232170426
43191CB00032B/1331